LOVE AGAIN BEFORE THE END OF TIME

I0164348

Vilanova de Gaia

Autobiographical poems and prose by Vilanova de Gaia Including poems by Vernique de Gaia

Excerpt from "The Green Kingdom" by Rachel Maddux, University of Tennessee Press, 1993

Disclaimer: Except for reference to a few authors, artists and acquaintances already discussed in the media, I am forced to test your credibility by disclaiming any relationship of what I have written about, to any person living or dead. It is purely coincidental, as is everything of which we speak, since it is only our own point of view. Yet someone with a litigious nature might decide to take offense and reduce me to penury in my attempt to". . . love again," which would be an all too ironic ending to this tale.

ISBN 9780990802808

Dedication

Dedicated to all the friends, family, and sometimes a good samaritan stranger, who have given me help and insights along the way, but especially to Vernique for a love that made me want more, and the women who have withstood my passionate exuberance in trying to ". . . love again before the end of time." My commiseration to all fellow travelers who have tempted the capricious fates with ". . . one more round."

Acknowledgement

Special thanks to my daughter, Katerina de Gaia, a published author now teaching English in Hawaii, who has given so much encouragement and literary support for many years in producing this tale. Thanks also to Terra's patience for the time I have stolen from our relationship to finish the book.

LOVE AGAIN BEFORE THE END OF TIME
Table of Contents

<u>TOLD IN TEN CHAPTERS</u> – *I'd prefer to have done it in five.*

Starting with a Disclaimer, Dedication and Acknowledgements, and ending with a biography of Vilanova – *My life of mental and physical adventure.*

CHAPTERS:

LOVE AGAIN BEFORE THE END OF TIME
Vilanova de Gaia struggles to maintain a passionate life.

After a fulfilling 47-year marriage, perhaps it's time to be self-sufficient. Yet, there's an inner voice that keeps urging me to ". . . love again before the end of time." Do I really want all the "baggage of life" that entails? It was one thing to start young and mold each other into the perfect partner, but now I would have to deal with a woman who is already set in her ways, as I am. These questions started to assail me after I had finished working through my initial grief at losing Vernique, with whom I had come to share almost every moment of my personal and business life.

In the final moments of her life, I learned that Vernique was not so afraid of dying as concerned about my future without her. She was no longer joking about leaving me to deal with our collection of bric-a-brac in the basement. She was hanging on to the last living thread of our richly entwined life, knowing that I was not yet ready to face up to the empty void when the thread snapped. Ironically, I was causing her to keep enduring all the pain of drowning from lung cancer, when she desperately needed to hold down the trigger-feed of the morphine overdose that would ease her over the edge. A compassionate spirit had released the morphine limits on the feed.

LEAVE ME BE! MOVE ON!
An ethereal message from Vernique to Vilanova
upon her death September 30, 2007

Leave me be as I was!
Love as you did for me
My very own true self.
Isn't it enough for us
That I am a part of you -

What I wove into you
Of my own pure essence?
She too may give this gift
Of her own pure essence
When you love for her self.

When I give her the time-honored "permission to die," I am freed of any guilt of "omission" as she murmurs that she is "fulfilled," that hand-in-hand, we reached our Shangri-la. We constantly re-affirm our love, but her unexpected exculpation of any doubt I might have of lifting her to the broader universe of fulfillment is like confronting Judgment Day and not to be found wanting.

With these last words, Vernique bequeaths a legacy to me and to my future relationships in dating, and ultimately in commitments to Giovanna and Terra, revealed in the following journey:

THE SOMETIME GIFT
Vilanova tries to give Giovanna a positive view of all the Vernique memorabilia, November, 2008

We learn to love
From how we experience it.
We learn to love
From loves that survive and grow.
After the death of "life's great love,"
Her image strewn about the house
Does not detract from a future amour
But marks the ability to love
Beyond anything that came before -
The sometime gift of "life's great love"
To the ones that follow.

This encourages me to want more - to love again before the end of time. After grieving, I start to date again, but finally admit to my sister Genevieve that this dating pales before the depth of what I have already experienced. Staying the course, while working through the challenges of a relationship between two very independent partners, Vernique and I achieved a harmonious serenity in "our trysting garden" of life, sharing each moment of our private and business lives.

Some of our most meaningful experiences came from working together. In New Orleans, Vernique was able to express her talents as a professional actress in producing and participating in numerous television and radio commercials in the advertising agency I directed. She was also one of the first graduates of Roy Cullen's pioneering television communications curriculum at the University of Houston. In creating a diverse range of copy for ads, she would really get pissed at me if I leaned too much on her eidetic memory, not allowing herself to be "wrung out" as if she were an early version of the yet-to-come personal computer.

She would never let me tell her friends about her ability to read every word on a page with one glance. As fast as she turned the pages, I would have sworn she was skim reading, until I chanced to read aloud to her a section she had reviewed a week before, when she casually picked up when I paused and she finished my reading from memory. Whether technical, prose or poetry, she had total recall for her lifetime. In our early years together in Houston, a close friend and successful young scriptwriter became aware of her ability to absorb so much of life as well as add back creatively. He jokingly suggested that I lock her up in solitary confinement for several years until I had a chance to catch up with her.

It almost seemed that the Creator had outdone himself, giving Vernique her exceptional IQ and talents, plus a striking beauty of alabaster skin, raven hair and large oval eyes with olive green irises. A lesser person would have been spoiled by it all. Although barely 5'2" with a 16" waist when we married, she certainly "walked tall" in the Texas vernacular. At 6'2", with strawberry blond hair and blue eyes, my physical attributes were in great contrast to Vernique's appearance.

In the Pacific Northwest, where we moved in 1976, our real satisfaction in working together came from extending our personal travel abroad and throughout the USA into selecting and marketing wines from European producers. Vernique soon proved that she had "eidetic taste buds" in evaluating or recalling wine flavors, styles, blends of different grapes and even blind recognition of Port Wine vintages. In the beginning, I felt so over-shadowed by her "natural bent" for wine expertise that I drove myself to gain equal recognition through experience. I soon became confident in dealing with long-term professionals in the business, never considering that the real challenge in losing her would be in my personal relationships of "loving again."

Falling back into the "dating game" later in life after losing a partner, the whole dance seems out-of-step with the life I knew, and a bit crazy. I worry about all kinds of superficial things. My close friends console me, pointing out that from what I have learned on this long voyage, my dates should be enraptured by fascinating tales of adventure or simply delightful interpretations of life's everyday experience. These would-be remoras (sucker fish) even urge me to tell them another *funny Vila story*." I notice that I have more patience and mellowness in making the compromises needed to form a strong and lasting relationship. Yet, my body may have suffered some physical ravages that could throw a wrench in the mating and physical affection side of the equation. This may ultimately trash the overall balance of mental and physical needs. I often wonder if I should just go on alone and be satisfied that I had one or two great relationships in the first innings.

Hopefully, my insights have been honed so that I can recognize the potential new mate without a long, careful courtship, because "the end of time" could be just around the corner. After trying a bit of the frustrating mating game, many of us who want to love again, recognize that we need to have a little courage. We need to be confident that our internal computer has been well-honed to recognize when *we should take another chance on love* and throw plodding caution to the wind.

What really made the commitment hang together for Vernique and I was our dedication to her baby daughter, left behind as her third husband sacrificed them to what he saw as his destiny to write the "Great American Novel." Becoming an alcoholic, he ended up losing everything – his dream, family, all of their meager savings and Vernique's diamond rings from her wealthy second husband. I sealed the compact by adopting Katerina.

MAKING IT EVEN BETTER

My relationship with Vernique became so good that I wanted to find another like it while there is still time. This was only an extension of living by the axiom of creating "a climate of potentiality," in which "I choose to think of myself as grappling, rather than buffeted," according to Rachel Maddux in "The Green Kingdom." I learned this climate can only be achieved by what Robert Musil in *"Der Mann Ohne Eigenschaften"(The Man Without Qualities)* called *"admitting all the possibilities, even those you haven't thought of yet."*

Of course, *". . . the man without qualities"* in the eye of society, is really Musil's tongue-in-cheek way of showing that his protagonist is really *". . . the man with qualities."*

My openness to what life has to offer is fundamentally framed by Musil's philosophy. He was a cult German writer who enlisted financial support for his writing career from members of a 1932 Musil-Gesellschaft foundation by Kurt Glaser in Berlin, This was an association of individuals contractually committed to a common goal: in this case, financial maintenance of the literary efforts of Musil, who even dunned his supporters for late payment. Such an unusual arrangement for an author did not detract from the achievement of Musil hitting on one of the great verities of life, even though it chased its own tail, *". . . admitting those possibilities you haven't thought of yet."*

In summing up a person's life, it has been pointed out that it isn't so much what was achieved, but what might have been – had we even known what to consider. We simply don't know what we don't know. An adventurous spirit at least minimizes the negative side of this equation and so enhances our short existence.

Making my task even more difficult in selecting the right future partner, I sought a life of passionate adventure, not settling for a cookie-cutter suburban existence, burying free spirits in stultifying conventions.

The Green Kingdom
Excerpt from Rachel Maddux poem in the book by the same name

The Green Kingdom lives in all men's hearts,
For it is less a place than a condition.

It is the promise born of man's longing that
His fate should bear relation to his own actions . . .

New Years Eve – *Celebrating Our Favorite Characters*

Vernique and I didn't merely react, but tried to reach beyond what's served up to us by life. We created satisfying interpersonal traditions, like bringing to life and love again our favorite characters of fact and fiction on New Year's Eve. For most of our 47 years together, opting out of compulsive and often drunken parties, we played the roles of favorite historical or mythical characters, the sole criteria being they inhabit the same time period. They might not have actually met, but we made it so, until we tired of the charade and slid "under the table" in blissful reverie.

That these intimate evenings became our most important private celebrations and axis of my life with Vernique was not foreseen at the time. It evolved more from finding something safer to do than drunkenly driving up the front door path, rather than the driveway after celebrating with friends. It was a natural course for Vernique to utilize her professional acting skills, having helped Nina Vance build the pioneering theater in the round, The Alley Theater, in Houston, Texas.

We dedicated the last half of the year to researching the lives of the characters we mutually decided to play. We came to the table on New Year's Eve in elaborate costumes, with a smattering of any foreign language our characters might have spoken, a knowledge of their experiences and preferences, including the cuisine of the time and what else was going on in the society and world about them. All our friends wanted to come and observe, as if we were putting on a performance, but that would have destroyed the intimate setting and spontaneity of how the evening unfolded. Small presents were given that showed creativity in appreciation for this captive moment, but could cost no more than $10 or $20.

As word got around of our celebration, we finally allowed a "Seattle Post-Intelligencer" columnist, Terry Taziola, to write a feature story. Vernique was pictured in a traditional full-length silk kimono, reclining on the living room sofa with a long cigarette holder held at arm's length. Overwhelming response poured in from all over the country to what was seen as an "enchanting approach to New Year's Eve."

Playing author and adventurer Luigi Barzini of Italy, I had recently returned from the grueling 1907 *Paris to Peking Auto Race*, giving an astonished Vernique, as the ever-youthful Jennie Churchill, a carved horn sailfish that "I caught in a mirage in the Gobi desert." It met the criteria of not costing more than $10, which the thrift shop, St Vincent de Paul, had for sale at $8.00. I carved a missing tail fin from a thin piece of black walnut.

The make-up alone for becoming Alexandre Dumas took an hour of pasting kinky hair around my forehead with spirit gum to mimic his mulatto appearance from being sired by a Jamaican mother. Vernique only had to don a full pink body suit to play Adah Menken, Dumas' longtime mistress, who astounded Parisians of the 1850s as the nude Lady Godiva crossing the theater stage on horseback. The gift of a lock of the hair covering her nude body was accompanied by the following card:

To Alexandre Dumas, Pere, from Adah Menken
(. . . written during her period of sturm and drang – also known as her "oh, woe, period," often erroneously described as "oh, no."

> *Alas, that as the breeze blows in the muses*
> *Landing upon his noble brow, his papers blow-*
> *And works of art the world never refuses*
> *Might 'round his chamber waft – and even go*
> *Where Saturn keeps lost tales of genius rare.*
>
> *Oh woe! Oh melancholy sad. Oh wreath of sere –*
> *Is there no way to clasp these jewels to my bosom?*
> *When inspiration strikes I am not there!*
> *I'll provide paper weights and hope he will use 'em*
> *When Talia and Clio lay their mysteries bare.*

Radiation & Distraction - *On the First^t Day of Radiation, my true love gave to me . . .*

Whether by reaffirming our bond through New Year's Eve characterizations or surviving stress caused by cancer treatment, I sought to make a difference where I could. When Vernique used up all the chemotherapy alternatives, including one of the latest experimental treatments, which was like self-torture, she finally agreed to radiation, which was not for remission, but to reduce the pain of advancing single cell carcinoma. Facing 21 days of radiation treatments, I thought to give her something to focus on and look forward to each day, a distraction that would blunt the ominous impact of daily radiation.

Borrowing from the Christmas ditty – "On the First Day of Christmas, my true love gave to me . . . ," I prepared a small "clue" poem each day hinting at the identity of the unique gift she was to receive. It turned out that the poems weren't nearly as much of a challenge to create as finding 21 gifts that would all live up to this elaborate and elongated charade. Each gift had to be something creative and special so she would look forward each day to receiving a well-conceived surprise after radiation. Selecting the next gift after using up the more obvious choices became more and more of a challenge when I passed the tenth gift. Ranging from $1.50 to $1,500, including a backward somersaulting monkey celebrating our African safaris, to flying in for dinner one of her dearly missed friends from when we lived in New Orleans.

MAINTAINING A PHYSICAL REALITY

How I related to Vernique was also very much conditioned by my commitment to maintain a physical reality in balance with mental intercourse. It was not to fame, riches, righteousness or humanity that I gave my allegiance, but an underlying human drive behind all these causes -- to seek a life of adventure and challenge, the path untrodden.

The desire to "work with my hands" also led me to periodically intern with three of the country's most talented sculptors: Ulric

Ellerhusen in Montville/Towaco, N.J., Prudence Leach and Joseph Putz in Houston, Texas.

Studying with Ulric, a year before his death at age 78 in 1957, five years before marrying Vernique in 1962, I was as much a caregiver as a student, but managed to learn basic techniques and the execution of large sculptures, such as the 8.5-ton, gold-leafed bronze statue of the Oregon Pioneer that rises 22 feet above the Oregon State Capitol building in Salem, of which Ulric had the original smaller work-up version overlooking the surrounding hills from patio outside his Montville home-studio. He was an early practitioner of ecological living, with all of the water used in the house collected in cisterns from the slate roof runoff.

Nearby, my small cottage with its huge artist's skylight could only be accessed by a short woodland path from the house at the top of the hill. It was the former secluded art studio of the portrait painter Alphaeus Philemon Cole, a New York City artist and son of renowned wood-engraver Timothy Cole. At the time of his death in 1988, at age 112 and 136 days, Alphaeus was said to be the ". . . *world's oldest verified living man.*" He was actively painting and exhibiting until age 103.

Worried that I might not be eating properly in my hideaway, as I finished the seven-mile trek home from work on my bicycle, the wife of the couple who currently owned the studio, frequently threw me a baked potato from the kitchen window of their modern home built into the side of the top of the hill, from where the path led to the cottage. Since they dubbed their home "Heather Hill House," I had some fun one weekend, completing an elaborate path-side sign for my own digs advising that you had arrived at "Heather Wee Cot,"which friends immediately called "Hither We Got."

I recently came across Alphaeus Cole's hand-written diary for the weekend of August 2-3, 1930, in the Archives of American Art in which he describes being lost with his wife Madge (sculptor Margaret Ward Cole) in the same woods that I lived in for a year: *"Passed a wakeful, miserable night beneath the trees. At dawn we found our way out of the woods. We had gone some mile or so out of our course and had to cross through a peach orchard and several fields . . . until we reached our cabin at 7am."* In those days, they had to bundle up to use the outhouse in the winter, since an addition providing space for a flushing toilet was only built in the 1950s.

From this, my visiting great aunt Effie emerged after a half an hour, exclaiming that she hadn't enjoyed a "resort" with such a fine broad brim since Colorado Springs, her hometown.

Joseph Putz was a Houston wood carver of high quality European style moldings and antique wood furniture repair for the finest homes and boutique hotels. He only took me on in my early twenties as a part-time student largely because of my Nordic blond looks, tall with a bronze tan and well-muscled physique from working in the oil fields during summers off from college. Evidently, I was what he wanted to look like, since he was short and gnome-like with an almost pointed head and somewhat bulbous nose.

While he had chiseled several large municipal sculptures in Germany and Austria, he had given up creative works to support himself with "no-nonsense" practical wood carving after the "Brits" blew off half the fingers of his right hand in the WWI. He sometimes raved about how stupid the "Brits" were in announcing their imminent attack by shelling the hell out of the German position; they only succeeded in depriving him of his stone carving ability.

He forced me to go through rigorous and tedious European training in wood carving before allowing me to try my hand at creative projects. So I learned to keep my tools sharp, make dozens of eggs and flowers out of increasingly harder woods and how to deal with wood grains attacked from all different directions. Like his Mexican helpers whom he weaned from their coarse Mexican style carving, I became proficient enough after several months to make classical figures and even a large skate fish that I still cherish. The last time I saw him, he was fighting cancer through drinking copious amounts of home-grown and made carrot juice, so that he had Beta Carotene poisoning, with his skin turning to the color of a carrot, which - with his pointed head - made him look like he had been carved out of the carrot itself.

Going over to the more familiar side of Putz wartime nemesis, I fell in love with British sculptor Prudence Leach, who made up for her skinny freckled looks with a captivatingly fey pixie nature. Yet there was nothing flighty about her; she was capable of grueling "live-ins" while casting her sculptures - building the plaster mold up on the clay statue a throw at a time over many days and nights while taking brief naps on army cots. Helping her with this task, we first established the seams for parting the cast by placing shim brasses into the clay to make the parting lines.

She had taken over a former Post Office in the Montrose area of Houston for her studio, and helped support herself by taking on a half-dozen students, including Vernique. After a week of almost living with the production of a making a bronze casting mold for a full-size sculpture called "Fallen Angels," Prudence and I were heading out for a relaxing dinner, when her psychotic ex-boyfriend leapt out of the shadows onto my back. I had always to be on the lookout for him, because like Cato laying in ambush for Inspector Clouseau in the *Pink Panther* movies, he was always trying to take me down with a surprise attack. But the day might come that he would feel frustrated enough to employ a knife or gun, not so easily thrown aside with disdain.

I had repeatedly warned Prudence that I was getting tired of his stalking, that she needed to be fair to him with courage to tell him to get lost, that their relationship was over – or ours might be over. Now, I used this as an excuse to approach Vernique the next time I was in the studio. We were soon dating, after I persisted, despite her ruse of playing the idiot by batting the long lashes of those large, oval-shaped green eyes. For a long time, I kept the more than life-size nose of Michaelangelo's David that she was sculpting, while the other five students focused on other parts of his anatomy, including what we called "his banana."

SEEING THE WORLD FROM INSIDE OUT

Vernique and I decided to set out on the first of of what turned out to be 50 trips abroad, almost as soon as our two children could be left safely in the hands of a house-sitter at home. We usually paid an employee from our office to stay at our house and look after everything. A daytime housekeeper managed the children during work hours.

We quickly learned how to get the most out of our travels. Not just to come prepared with knowledge of the region buoyed by anticipation, but to stay at least five days in one location to get some local feeling for the area before going on to the next. Our day trips were limited to 70 km, building intersecting pieces into a web of 150 km radii intersecting each other as we moved across the country in successive trips.

Our first trips were to Spain, including following the road on the much celebrated pilgrimage to Santiago de Campostela in Galicia, during which I had prepared more of a romantic than spiritual demonstration. What was meant to publicly show my great love for Vernique, and did – indeed - draw hundreds of enthralled Spanish couples to my side, but - at the same time - crowded Vernique out to the edges, convinced – as she later scolded me – for doing this all for the benefit of my ego rather than any love for her.

Without her being aware of my plans, I had secreted aluminum-crafted armor, in a separate suitcase, along with a 16-foot banner, claiming *"A Que Vernique es las mas Hermosa de Todas!"* over intersecting knights' lances. We arrived at the infamous, Roman-built bridge of Quiñones at Lugo, where this spike-collared knight challenged all other knights to admit "his lady is the fairest of them all," the gist of my banner in Spanish. I had a local couple, whom I had filled in on my scheme, distract her attention at the *Taverna of Quiñones* on the far side of the bridge. I strapped on my armor and helmet, erected the banner over the bridge with local teenage conscripts and sent a message to the tavern for them to return with Vernique. Then, I started stopping cars on the one-way bridge, demanding they sign the banner in agreement to my challenge before proceeding, but didn't kill anyone, as did Quiñones (beyond the rules of chivalry), or get killed or arrested in the process. Demonstrating their own romantic Spanish character, no one refused or threatened me with jail, but exclaimed why they hadn't thought of this before some amorously crazy Americano. When the police finally arrived, they could only go along with the celebratory atmosphere, since there were already so many cars parked all over the place and so many signatures on the banner attesting to Vernique's beauty, as if she could even be seen in the crowd, while I was being hugged and kissed by women and their partners alike. Ego, yea!

After seeing most of Europe for pleasure, our wine importing business took us back to see it from the inside out, not as a tourist but from the point-of-view of a resident in a business relationship. As wine importers, we also traveled throughout the U.S. to promote the wines we selected from wineries all over Europe.

A FADO... TO PORTUGAL
FROM THE NEW WORLD
by Vernique in 1975, after peace in the "Flower Revolution"
Our first trip to Portugal, which seduces into importing wine.

A barefoot lady in a pastel gown
Whose tender upper lip
Is shadowed by black down –
She wears a wooden yoke
The Arabs left behind,
And walks a winding road
Across the trembling ground.

Do not mistake the smoothness of her cheek –
The shining eyes, the mane of glossy hair,
For youth – wait 'til you hear her speak ...
Her voice is husky with her thousand years.

Wherever the Atlantic's curling foam
Touched on a faraway shore, there she walked –
And carried the curious language of her home
To mingle with the cries of alien birds –
Leaving her high-arched, slender print on foreign sand.

This is the legacy –this, the antique lace
She wraps around her head when evening comes
And charcoal burners add their pungent trace
Of wood smoke and sardines to the warm air.

Lady, the road is long and the race is old.
Jewels once sparkled on her well-kept hands,
But they were slowly sold to pay the bills –
Only a whisper of her name in far-off lands
Remains to show what treasures once were hers.
All the known world was hers, and the unknown
Became her garden which she tended well –
But when the trees she planted were all grown
They bore their fruit for other hands to pick.
(Well, nothing on earth was ever that secure,
Even the earth itself has played her false.)

Resting a moment beside the familiar sea,
She gazes wearily across its heaving waste
And mumbles to her self a litany:
Macao, Angola, Brazil and Mozambique –
The errant children whom her name once graced.

Traveling to Ravello on the Amalfi coast of Southern Italy in 1994, we visited the famous Villa Cimbrone built on ancient Roman ruins in the 12th Century and which became the "noble perch" of the British aristocracy and literati of the Bloomsbury Club. It was also noted as the elopement hideout of Greta Garbo and Leopold Stokowsky.

Faced with the proximity of Vernique's death, we could no longer afford literary license -- the "smart or cultured" appeal of this oft-quoted inscription on the garden tombstone – that all too soon became banal and posturing.

**"LOST TO A WORLD IN WHICH I CRAVE NO PART
I SIT ALONE AND COMMUNE WITH MY HEART
PLEASED WITH MY LITTLE CORNER OF THE EARTH
GLAD THAT I CAME, NOT SORRY TO DEPART"**

Chiseled in stone at the Villa Cimbrone garden in Ravello, Italy, this note of having a "safe and serene refuge" against a sometime alienating world was written by neoteric poet Catullus around 60 BC. It finally came "home" in this garden, overlooking the dramatic Amalfi coast, when D.H. Lawrence wrote this version as a memorial to Lord Grimthorpe who owned the Villa.

Before visiting this part of Italy, we became very familiar with the history of the area, having played the character parts at the most recent of our New Year's Eve charades of two 20th Century patricians who met at Villa San Michele on the Isle of Capri. Made famous by *The Story of San Michele*, written by the villa owner, Dr. Axel Munthe, whose part I played for the period in 1919-20 when he was the unwilling landlord at the Villa San Michele of the flamboyant Luisa, Marchesa Casati, played by Vernique. Dr. Munthe was a serious Swedish-born physician who almost sacrificed his life to help during a cholera epidemic in Naples, at which time he bought San Michele on Capri, setting up a medical practice in Rome to be near this renovation of many decades.

From the moneyed-aristocracy, our characters both had a love of "pet" wild animals in common, although we would have had to raid the local zoo to include such diverse pet situations as Axel drinking with Billy, his alcoholic baboon, and Luisa parading behind two leashed cheetahs, her neck festooned with a writhing, live snake necklace. She was also famed as the "hostess" to the *Ballets Russes* and, in all ways, lived up to her desire ". . . to be a living work of art."

Our travels kept on through many surgeries and regular chemotherapy. Never allowing the constant pain to throw her off course, she continued to travel despite knowing that we would be seeing more of the Emergency Room on each trip both local and abroad.

Some of our most exotic travels were to Africa, Egypt and the Orient. We had some close calls with her health, but managed to stay out of hospitals, though the loose pills in the bush-doctor's pocket mixed with lint were surprisingly effective. Was it a "placebo effect?" They had no expiration date or even a label to confirm what they were.

Egypt was always intriguing, and we even had some fun with trivia learning Arabic numerals from the license plates on cars as we drove along with our guide, similar to the games we played as children on long car trips from home. Picking up a bit of the language became helpful in many ways. I was able to say in Arabic how much I enjoyed Egypt while handing my passport with "backsheesh" of a 10 Egyptian pound note inside (US4$) over the heads of a crowd of irate German tourists trying to check-in their "lost" reservations at the Old Cataract Hotel in Aswan, featured in the Agatha Christie movie, "Death on the Nile." We got the best suite in the house with a 20-foot wide veranda overlooking a string orchestra playing at the edge of the Nile. Visiting the Egyptian tombs while staying in Luxor, Vernique composed this poem:

SILENT NOW IN THE SUN
By Vernique in Egypt, 1989

> *The emptiness*
> *Shimmers with the face of God,*
> *Sweep of sand shifting,*
> *Eternally changing, eternally the same*
> *The sky*
> *Shines where the sand ends,*
> *Where the shadows meet,*
> *Where we cannot go.*
> *Here*
> *In the immensity,*
> *We build our house of death*

Where there is no life
Rustling in the sand.

Kites soar above the ruins
Where priests walked,
Where love and hate,
Power and pride,
Lived their long ago day.
On crumbling columns
Scratched lines speak,
"I lived...I had a name...
I cried out to God."
Silent now, in the sun.

Whatever we drop in this dry sand
Will be preserved...
Under it, the artifacts
Of 5,000 years survive:
Delicate turquoise and lapis,
Fragments of pottery,
A tiny alabaster cat...
And my wristwatch crystal -
All will be there forever,
All the same under the sand.

Before going to Egypt, my friends with a horse farm helped me brush up on the basics of riding, at least enough that I wouldn't get my foot caught in the stirrup, providing I stayed away from unpredictable Arabian stallions, which of course was my first selection for galloping off into the Sahara with a guide who was somehow able to recover my eyeglasses from the sand. Vernique very bravely managed to get back to the hotel on her own as it became obvious that we had gone too far to return until morning after the intervening sandstorm and not having cell phones to use in Egypt in 1989. We actually spent the night in a Tuareg camp about which I wrote the following poem.

MOUNTAINS IN THE DESERT
From Vilanova for all who are open to life – Egypt 1989

Blue-mantled Tuaregs riding swift camels,
Lithe snakes weaving patterns down the dunes,
The gritty sandstorm isolating us in our tracks.

All this immensity makes us feel miniscule
In the vastness of the cathedral silence . . .
Yet magnified by our singular presence.

Evening comes. The fiery globe of sun
Melts down to an opalescent reflection
In the cooling sand where it solidifies
And is captured by the night
That throws up counter-point of moon
And stars, giving substance
To the fathomless eternity above.

In the distance, shadow-striped tents
Emerge among the silhouette
Of bandy-legged palm trees.
The night-blue Tauregs welcome us
More by subtle signs than strange words.
Safe as guests within the sacred circle,
We are fair game to nature
And all human madness
Beyond the tented fastness,
Taking adventure
With the frisson of threatening forces
That always lurks outside.

VERNIQUE – LIVING EVERY DAY
TO FULFILLMENT
"Six months to live" that became our seven best years

After 40 years of our marriage that had solidified through all the challenges of two people with high expectations, Vernique was diagnosed with Stage 3 ovarian cancer and latent lung cancer with a prognosis of about six months to live, unless she fell into the 10% that might survive another five years or so with a lot of surgery, chemotherapy and radiation.

She contemplated going to Oregon to embrace euthanasia, then shoved the ugly "cancer" word out of her vocabulary and we both focused on extracting the most out of every minute of the remaining time together. This was to last seven years. Within two months after ovarian surgery, we interrupted her initial round of chemotherapy for the first of four safaris in Kenya. We had always planned to go to Africa, but selecting and maintaining our foreign wine imports kept us focused on Europe.

As the illness progressed into her liver and suffocating double lung cancer, we were always able to look the long-faced pitying stares in the eye and truly declare that *"Oh, no! These are the best years of our lives because we are paying attention to every moment."*

Selecting Africa in answer to the surgeon's question of what she wanted to do with, perhaps, only six months to live, Vernique survived long enough to take a three-week safari in Kenya every other year from 2000 to 2007, when she died at the end of September. At that point, I took the charity that developed from these safaris to a new level of helping local children in villages surrounding the wildlife reserves in Kenya. The project became Kenyan Kids on Safari (KKOS), www.kidsonsafari.org. It proved to promote the kids' self esteem as well as helping their communities view wildlife conservation in a viable balance against the threat to native crops and cattle.

Perhaps, KKOS would be a better arena to employ all my energy than being drained off in trying to love again. In the end, I struggle to have both, which I try to reason out in this poem:

TO GIVE MY BEST, FOR CERTAIN
TO LOVE AGAIN, PERCHANCE
BEFORE THE END OF TIME
Vilanova, July 11, 2008

Last night, a thrilling epiphany.
As a phoenix rising from the ashes
From my half-century love for Vernique -
Living, loving, sharing everything
With my best friend of a lifetime.

Left without her physical presence
My heart cried out for another chance.
Being loved so well for a long time
Diverted all energy of mind and soul
To an addiction in seeking continuation
Of what took most of my life to build.
Writing frequent poems of love and joy
So overwhelming in their constancy
To charm, but baffle the best of friends.

Suddenly, I perceived my romantic folly
That could just as easily turn to anguish
Investing all remaining time and energy
Into a chimera of my love for Vernique.
Unlikely to ever be recreated
Before the end of time.
Now, my path lies clearly drawn
Shifting focus before "the end of time"
To the best I can give, - can share
Of wisdom that has tempered me
During life's fulfilling adventure.
And, who knows?

Taking this path of giving for certain
I may encounter love, per chance
With another companion along the way.

Now, to re-invent myself from her ashes -
Her love for African nature and people.
To help give the children of this Eden
More than bread, health and welfare -
A chance to find what makes life worth living
In their own "backyard" game reserves.

This Eden, the whole world treasures,
But few can afford a safari,
Much less the African children.
Where the community of life
Still husbands nature in the balance
For African Kids on Safari.

While Vernique struggled on with life through chemotherapy, radiation and the experimental drugs she ultimately encountered, from the outset she had a great dread of being a bed-ridden invalid, or being tied to a wheelchair where you seem to vanish from focus, as people in front of you converse over your head. She only used a wheelchair at rare times when she needed to conserve her energy for moving about normally upon arrival at her destination. Even for the last few weeks when she was bed-ridden, her fantastic mind and total recall of everything she read or heard peopled her physically inert world. She could quote an entire universe of art, but never did it for show. It was part of the natural flow of her conversation, carried on a gentle breeze of "poetry" that never slapped you in the face or went beyond its welcome.

She shunned being called an "intellectual" – always true to her younger self in appreciating all life had to offer – wanting gentle sex even up to her dying moment as noted in this poem:

OH, THE DAYS OF WILD ABANDON

... a tribute to sexuality by Vilanova, March 23, 2008

Keep your urges in rein
Until the body follows
The spiritual lead of the brain
For love gives landscape to lust
That never cheapens memories.

Looking up into your eyes
Your naked body grooved in mine
The ends of your hair brushing my face
Swinging breast barely grazing my chest.
All dreams to cherish from a long, long love
That went so deep, so unfettered
That it is always with me.

Oh, the days of wild abandon!
Will they ever come again
Before too old to go the course?
Not being one for casual sex –
(Erika Jong – au contraire)
I must not rush the course,
But trust good counsel of the brain
To honor mutual fulfillment
In days of wild abandon.

Her wonderful intellect, appreciation for balance in art as well as nature, and an ever-present sense of humor shielded her in a private world of her own making, yet made her even more vulnerable to the greater loss from her greater interplay in life itself when her body received the life-term prison sentence with no chance for parole.

Then some anonymous authority decided to test her stamina, to challenge her will to live by repeated taunts with false firing squads of chemical and radiation "bullets" that only succeeded in injuring another part of her body, as if it would trim down her "tree of life" limb-by-limb. In moments of desolation, she was almost pushed to take control and cut down the trunk of her tree of life itself. Only to be thrust back on life's treadmill through her great joy in even the smallest continuity of things, as if her veins were infused through so many tendrils in a sort of a self-perpetuating osmosis of the body and soul that would take hold and keep her going.

Most of this was inwardly generated from her vast layers of memory and reserves, a self-sufficiency that only needs a slight balance of good friends and loving husband on the outside. Sometimes "we" could reach down to walk hand-in-hand with her through this valley of the "shadow of death," but only fleetingly, and never sufficient to blot out those solitary moments when she would become overwhelmed with silent desperation and a sense of the futility of surviving each challenge to her life and the growing weight of the finality of it all, like an enlarging tumor that would envelop her whole self.

Yet her great joy in life, and above all her deep faith in God, ultimately lifted her back up into the light and kept her going through all the twists and turns, all the life-threatening moments when she faced the insurmountable wall of her body's prison. Truly God loved and admired her faith and persistence in overcoming all obstacles while caught in this prison garden maze where there is no physical way out, but only through the mind.

I wrote "On The Plateau" as a tribute to Vernique, having friends help me achieve acceptable translations into Portuguese and Italian for reciting while spreading her ashes in the vineyards that she visited yearly over 32 years. The most touching ceremony was at Cabanon in the Altrepo Pavese of Northern Italy just below Pavia. She was given the ultimate honor of "resting" alongside the grave of the revered father and founder of the winery behind the consecrated, native stone chapel on the property. Most moving of all, a dozen agricultural workers, dressed in their crimson Cabanon work-shirts, sang in Italian commemorating her passing, songs that I heard as if lilting poetry from Vernique's spirit. Even these workers were moved to tears, which turned to wine as we returned to the owner's nearby house to celebrate her life with some of the wines she most loved.

ON THE PLATEAU

Vilanova's tribute to Vernique, five months after her death, February 28, 2008

*You left me fulfilled
At a place where it is just as easy to die,
Just as easy to join you in oblivion or renewal
As it is to go on.*

*On Where?
Where friends and family
Engulf me in a moment of their lives.
Where I can leave something behind as a hymn
To our life together.
Where no obstacles can deter me,
Can stress me, or even matter –
Because it is just as easy to die.*

*Like the spirit that soared from your body
I am free of earthly cares
Meeting the fates with a smile
As I pass them by
On this plateau between life and death.*

*Meeting you, as I used to in the morning
When you rounded the foot of the stairs
Feeling pure rapture in your being.
The soft butterfly touch of your slim hand in mine,
We turn aside to join another day,
Another reprieve from the cancer you held at bay
Through pure will—and a little chemo.*

*Now, a comforting breeze has swept aside
The pain and anguish of your death.
You are beside me forever
With all the sensory joy that memory can conjure –
And an occasional haunting to our delight.*

"On The Plateau", Vilanova's tribute to Vernique, translated into the following Portuguese and Italian versions, recited while scattering her ashes in the vineyards of our wine producers in those countries.

NO PLANALTO

- a Vernique, cinco meses apos a sua morte (to Vernique, five months after her death)

(Portuguese translation of "On the Plateau" in English above)

Deixaste-me com uma vida completada
Num lugar onde é tão fácil morrer,
Tão fácil juntar-me a ti no céu ou na renovação,
Como é fácil continuar.

Continuar para onde?
Para onde amigos e familia
Me abrace num momento das suas vidas.
Onde eu posso deixar algo como que um hino
À vida que passamos juntos.
Onde obstaculos não me deteem,
Nem me afligem, nem mesmo me importam -
Porque é tão fácil morrer.

Como o espírito que voou para cima de seu corpo
Estou livre de cuidados terrestres
Olhando os fados com um sorriso
Quando os enfrento
Neste planalto entre vida e morte.

Encontrar-te, como usei para pela manhã
Quando você arredondou o fundo das escadas
Pura êxtase sentindo em seu ser.
O toque de borboleta macio de sua mão esbelta em meu,
Nós desviamos unir outro dia,
Outra suspensão do câncer você segurou à distância
Por pura força de vontade - e um pequeno quimo.

Agora, uma brisa confortante veio aligeirar
A dor e a angústia da tua morte.

Estás para sempre junto a mim
Com toda a alegria sensória que memória pode evocar -
E, por vezes, uma aparição para nosso encantamento.

Por Vilanova de Gaia, 28 de Fevereiro, 2008 translated into Portuguese by my dear friends Luis & Luisa Lourenço

To Vernique, the most important reward that she received by going on with a full life in spite of cancer was the great honor Luis and Luisa Louenço, the owner's of the renowned Dão Portuguese winery, Quinta dos Roques, bestowed on her. They saw that all of her dedication and skills in promoting their wines, and other fine wines from all over Portugal for over 30-plus years, were properly recognized. At a stately ceremony in a celebrated Portuguese chapel in Viseu, she was the first woman from the US to be made a *Confrade of the Confraria do Vinho do Dão* (the highest membership in the brother/sister-hood of the wine region that dates back to Roman times). The Lourenços will always be our *Portuguese family.*

SULL'ALTOPIANO
A Vernique, a cinque mesi dalla sua morte (to Vernique, five months after her death)
(Italian translation of "On the Plateau" in English above)

Mi hai lasciato compiuto
In un luogo dove e' facile morire,
Facile raggiungerti, nell'oblio o nel rinascimento
Cosi com' e' il prosceguire nel cammino.

Dove amicizia e famiglia
Ti avvolgono in un attimo delle loro esistenze.
Dove posso lasciare il ricordo di un inno
Alla nostra vita trascorsa.
Dove nessun ostacolo mi distolga,
Possa inquetarmi oppure importi -
Perche e'altrettanto facile morire.

Cosi come l'alito che esalo' dal tuo corpo
Io sono libero da capricci terreni
Vivo sorridendo al fato
Come un viandante che passa.
Sull'altopiano che sta' fra vita e morte.

Reincontrandoci come usavamo nel mattino,
Il tuo piede che toccava lieve le scale -
Pura estasi esistenziale.
Il tocco lieve come di farfalla,
Le tue mani scarne sulle mie,
Il cammino verso un'altro giorno
Strappato al male che cosi bene tenevi a baia
Con pura volonta' – e un po' di terapia.
Una riassicurante brezza ha spazzato via le
nebbie
Dell'angosciante pena.
Sei con me per sempre
Con la gioia intatta dei sensi
Che la memoria congiura a evocare –
Occasinale riapparizione della nostra gioia.

by Vilanova de Gaia, 28 Febbraio 2008
translated into Italian by my great friend Giovanni Springolo

WHERE THEIR SPIRIT ARMS EMBRACE ME
Vilanova's epiphany while flying to San Francisco, May 8, 2008

Oh, Vernique you fooled us all
Found the realm not bound by time
As the Hopi Indians knew
Along with J. B. Priestly.

Gazing from the airplane window -
Suddenly, emerging from the clouds

Showing where I've been, where I am,
Where I'm going, all in one moment
That will last forever now I'm where
Their spirit arms embrace me.

Now, friends give me open sky
Without knowing, or do they?
Wanting me to find it for myself
The only way to truly enfold life,
Seeing that their warmth of spirit
Is greater than anything else
I could find in earthly pleasures.

Pure gift of these unfettered minds
Beyond any love I could imagine,
Solitary yet surrounding -
As riding into the Sahara.
Realizing the spirit world is peopled
By all who care and were cared for
Less alone than with my mirrored self.

How came this to my thoughts?
With time to pause before the flight
I found myself musing --
That I had just met my two selves
Passing each other in the walkway.
One somewhat self-absorbed
Busily on his well-anchored way
Sure Vernique was always there.
Never admitting that her death
Would really happen in his life,
So constantly she fooled the fates.

My other self still evolving,
Surrounded by a welcoming aura
Where ever I go, opens gates
To what's there, but oft goes unseen.
Vernique creates a small universe

For me, so that I can manage
Without her physical presence.
Now this universe comforts me –
Is not closed, has no doors or gates,
Admits all, needs no defenses,
Because nothing can hurt me more
Than her absent being, now joy
In communing with her spirit –
Embraced by all my universe.

CHAPTER FIVE – ADDING ANOTHER DIMENSION

VERNIQUE'S POETRY

Appreciating my slice of a "passionate" life with Vernique, honed my desire to "love again before the end of time." I spent most of a lifetime entranced by the poetry of Vernique's yearning for a meaningful life that we both shared in fulfilling. Fortunately, she kept a packet of the poetry and short stories she had written since a young girl, of which follow relevant pieces, in addition to those poem used in earlier chapters giving an enhanced dimension to our travels:

I NEVER CEASE TO LOVE THIS WORLD
By Vernique, 1955-1960

In her mid twenties, as if foreseeing her death,
Vernique already felt the pressure to reap the most out of life.
The "seers" prophecy of " three-score and ten" (70 years) was
close to her 72 year lifespan.

Wide-eyed child that I am,
I never cease to love
This world. I want to cram
The swift flight of a dove,

Black cliffs against the sky,
Swallows lined up in rows
On telephone wires, dry
Leaves blown as the wind grows

Into my memory.
For the time will come when

I am gone – seers decree
Just three-score years and ten.

Three-score years – little time
To behold beauty sublime.

THE LIGHTED WINDOWS
OF OTHER PEOPLE'S HEARTS
by Vernique in Houston, Texas,. 1961

I have been all my life
Standing in the rain,
Pressing my nose against the lighted windows
Of other people's hearts.

There is the yellow circle of enchantment,
There the warm fire and laden oak-beamed board;
The magic bread and salt they share of laughter
And song, the braided rugs upon the floor.

I COULD NOT DIE IN APRIL
by Vernique in her early teens. 1949

A prophetic thought, ultimately challenged on April 18, 2007
when Vernique barely survived congestive heart failure
only to succumb to lung cancer on September 30, 2007

I could not die in April,
(In my own hemisphere)
when the young year's first flowers
Are timidly appearing,
When the rain is as fresh as the tears of a child,
And the wind is crushed green mint.
In March – yes, I could bear to leave this world.
In August, too – I would not grieve at dying –

But April? When the tiny, tremulous details
That finish the Earth's raw edges
Are new and still to be savored – Not I!
Not 'til the rain is cold and leaves have fallen.

CHAPTER SIX – HEALING LOVE

HELENE, REACHING A PLATEAU OF FRIENDSHIP

From the beginning in October 2007, Helene protected me from myself, while lifting me up from the black hole of grief. She didn't let me destroy our great friendship by stepping over the line with even one dalliance. The gentle touch of her palm against my chest kept me at bay. Long walks together in the "free-run" park with her dog "Troy" gave vent to my wounds. Certainly, her warmth and affection helped me endure the recent loss of Vernique. She gently endured my outpouring of lust to help me walk through this seemingly impenetrable forest. I sufficed with the European friendship kiss on each check and an occasional hug, but never as lovers as she played cache-cache (hide-n-seek) with her lips – the scope of one poem.

Of medium height with raven black hair, her early ballet training and rock climbing had endowed her with a purposeful walk, almost like a stalking panther. The intensity of her dark irises either entranced or made you want to look away, but you are soon put at ease with her effervescent gaiety and French-speaking manner of making a rose petal pucker of her lips.

SEE HOW SHE FLIES

Sharing "a moment of flight" driving to the ballet with Helene, followed by a Spanish dinner at my festively decorated table, and hearing of her own youthful memories as a child in an apple tree. - Vilanova, March 2008

> *See how she flies,*
> *How she conjures up a ballet of birds in the sky,*
> *A thousand strong,*

Soaring, swooping along the waterfront buildings,
Parting and then together again in their dance
Of joy at being alive – and together.

She how she flies
This Helene who draws pictures with nature in the sky.
No matter, whether it really happened.
It happened to our delight – in being together,
This preview to another soaring evening at the ballet
As the goal of our drive.

See how she flies,
This multi-coloured bird – a protected specie
That cannot be captured
But can give me the gift of a moments flight
Always knowing that I have flown with her.

Vea cómo ella vuela,*
This pájaro, celebrating las mañanitas,
The "mornings" of our delight – together.
With a Piñata, small woven birds in the stag-horn chandelier
Helene, bringing grand vinos españoles – to bond
With Oaxacan tamales, mole poblano and Cuitlacoche.

She how she flies,
As a young bird in her native Quebec
Gorging her exuberant being in a tree of apples
She ruffles her tiny wing feathers in anticipation
Of such winged migrations as we share together.
Thanks to Vernique who gave me flight.

Translation – "See how she flies, this bird, celebrating the mornings of our birth," Las Mañanitas – Mexican birthday song

ALAS, WHEN BIRNAM WOOD
WOULD COME TO DUNSINANE!

(MacBeth plays a joke on Vilanova's madness)
Vilanova - March 23, 2008

Bird lice or bird lust -
Both make me itch.
I laugh at myself,
As teen-like hormones
Rack my composure,
Crowding my thoughts,
With maddening desire
For this innocent bird.
Arab men blame the woman,
For their own intemperate urges.

Alas, my cover is exposed,
Desire hidden in the forest
I brought to "Duns-Helene"
Approaching the core of her citadel
Bonded by our mutual attraction
Of mind and purpose, as well as–
For flair in style of action and being.

To discover this rare specie
At the plateau of love's fulfillment –
Rising from Vernique's ashes as a phoenix
Sent for me to continue
The pure joy in my life
With such a woman to share it,
If only for a moment.

Oh, stronger it tantalizes –
'Til one satisfies the itch
or lets it fly away forever.
So what's the culmination
Of overwhelming desire?
(Quell the pulsing blood
That would hurry it!)
Is it ultimate affirmation
Or the end to what exists?
So scratch, scratch, scratch
Rather than chance
Being lost in Birnam Wood.

COME, WALK IN THE GARDEN OF EDEN

*Vilanova to Helene-- sharing another moment at her home
that turned into one of the most joyous of my life. April 2, 2008*

Come,
Walk in the Garden of Eden
With all your senses unleashed
Where a soft "jambo" wakes you
To cookies and tea
And we're off
On Safari

Morning chill
Fiery pink sunrise
Greets animals and man
Emerging from burrows
Others returning
From nightly stalks

Air so fresh
So invigorating
The way it always should be.
Let nature lead us into the day
What unexpected pleasure!
To share with you

A lion feeding on a buffalo kill
Brought down by his lionesses.
Hyena cubs cautiously peering out
Then falling back down the hole.
Rainbow colored birds playing chase
As we search along the dirt road
Then go bumping off through the bush.
To track the far ranging cheetahs.

We sit all day long observing
The family life of elephants

Until they become so used to us
They almost bump our vehicle.
Cautious mothers letting their young
Come closer, to make their own Safari
Inspecting the strange box of humans
That adds to their own diversity.

How healthy most of the animals!
Not shaggy or dejected in a zoo.
But welcoming or indifferent
And sometimes even hostile
To our visiting them at home
They share their real lives in nature.
A gift beyond anything imagined.

LEAVE YOUR YOUNG HEART OPEN TO IT. .

for Helene who inspires me, Vilanova, April 14, 2008

Love well-traveled, not indiscriminate –
But true and straight as an arrow,
Although scored with years of flight,
Can still shoot to the heart
As from the bow of a Du Guesclin.

Do not discount the frazzled feathers
Of this shaft of countless sorties
Past the hearts of applauding beauties
To the one true love of its chivalry,
Then rounding out its journey
With one last bout at your nimble feet.

Lifting you up from life's random wounds
To the heights where you were meant to soar.
Never to be winged again by a warped arrow
But soaring, soaring into the infinite blue.

Leave your young heart open to it
For it sings through the air to its mark
Louder still for every frazzled feather
Than from the bow of any younger knight.
Making its mark of sheer joy for a moment
Imbedded in your heart's lifetime.

NOTHING LEFT BUT A DREAM OF LOVE

Vilanova's Spring thoughts, April 15, 2008

I will not die of a broken heart,
-- could die of a bursting heart.
So filled with love of life am I,
April Fool of new-sprung earth
Caught in the season of rebirth
Teasing the moment of my return
Below new shoots of dew-trod grass.

Leaving a thousand bent blades
'Neath my barefoot dancing legs
Exhorting wind-whistling music to –
Sing a lusty tune,
Drive me mad,
Roll once more in damp green,
Bursting apart with such joy
Nothing left but a dream of love.

BURSTING WITH PASSIONATE SERENITY

To Helene from Vilanova, this gift of a cello, April 17, 2008
"Passionate Serenity" seems a conflict of terms, but it is so.

Mornings – with Vernique
When I meet her at the foot of the stairs
Always feeling pure rapture in her being,
Did not die with her
Or diminish our love
Finding communion with Vernique's soul.

Another beautiful Leo Woman
That only most opportune chance
Could put near the foot of my stairs,
Continuing the rapture each day
That fills me with such stolen joy
That I cry out for my good fortune.

Then, if I can do her a kindness
A small gift for her many talents,
It's nothing to what she has given,
That though gently platonic
Has allowed me to maintain
A sense of rapture in each day.

With this "early birthday" gift
I hope to return a bit of the same joy
That lifts me above the chasm of grief.
Listening – (and being remembered)
Where ever I am.
Listening –
To her stroke a vibrant tone
And bursting with "passionate serenity".

FRISSON OF NATURE
Vilanova, April 21, 2008

Upon seeing the photo of Helene scaling a 200-ft sheer ice wall.

At the ice wall you overcome fear with mastery,
Almost – or where the exhilaration?
Clutched by the giant wave my timing is perfect,
Nearly – but that's the thrill of it all.
For mastery of nature can never be complete,
As she herself is a fickle master.

Beyond oft-used words - love, passion, friendship –
I am encompassed by a "Vilaship" for you.
So melded into your form, action and spirit
To have that frisson of nature,
Where no mastery can totally prevail
Where I am so enthralled by your being
That nature smiles and winks
At mere human absurdity
To ever ascend to total mastery of it all.

GIFT OF HAUNTING SPLENDOR
Vilanova to Helene at the close of April 2008

Glancing at Helene's profile next to me at the ballet.

To have seen your profile in repose,
Haunting splendor fills my mind
With the serenity of woman-child
In the wisp of smile and shaded eye
Dozing off to strands of ancient music
So tired you could not regret the slide
Into a moment of peaceful reverie.

'Tis a stolen gift beyond compare,
Beyond any picture I have of you
Captured forever in my memory.
Seeing your profile once and again
On the pillow next to my own cheek
Wishing, as I lie in dream-like state
That apparition might be reality.

UNTIL I AM WITH YOU
Vilanova, April 22, 2008

If I can touch you in the morning
When you are still warm from bed
By reading my email message
With a smile or little laugh
Then I am with you.

If I can add dimension to your day
With just a word or two
Letting you know that I care
About everything good and bad
Then I am with you.

With you in mind gives such sheer glory
That it causes me to celebrate
With even more thoughts of you
Helping me to endure
Until I am with you.

MY GARDEN SIGHS WITH RELIEF
Vilanova, before drifting into desperate sleep, April 30, 2008

Enough with pink, white and lavender
I want yellow, bright glowing yellow

That mirrors the warm sun in my yard
But it must be fiery, rich yellow
Not the pallid, sickly, deathly yellow
That left no sun for Dostoyevsky.

In my wild garden, trees and plants
Became entangled with neglect,
Strangled in suffocating embrace.
Now they sigh in unrestrained relief
As I give each plant back its space
Opening corridors that delight my eye.

I must get rigorous, prune grape vines
Climatis and ivy that festoon the house.
They worm their way into every crack
To see if I will curb their wanton growth.
Testing me to see if I still have the will,
The pleasure to bring it all back in thrall.

Helene, I want to share it all with you,
Every joy in what I think and do.
But you have so much going on
That it's amazing we have any time.
Though we reap so much delight
In the stolen time we are together.

MORE LIKE A CHEETAH
Vilanova, May1, 2008

More like a cheetah
Than sultry lioness
With grace of limbs
Lithe in movement
Bounding forward
On thrusting legs,
How my heart leaps!

Seeing you
Dressed for the kill,
Jealous thoughts,
Extreme beauty
Stalking alone
Worrying
That some other cat
Would run long-side
Of such an attraction.

To love such a cat,
My whole soul
Shivers in sight
Of the black trim
At your bosom.
Chaffing, chaffing
To run with you
Through deep grass
Of Masai Mara –
Touching flanks.

FOR FEAR OF NOT KNOWING OF YOU
Vilanova to Helene May 3, 2008

Alone and isolated in the black corner of my world
The vortex of the infinite would swallow me up
Should anything even slightly hurtful happen to you.
Who knows or cares to call me in an emergency?
How could my commitment lay claim on family
Unaware of the joy your image bring to every day
That hardly knows what you reciprocate for me?

Strange, to be brought down to earth by practicality
Of finding a way to notify Helene in case of emergency
Though my daughter would take charge of salient matters

Not to place another demand on the fetters of you life
Only that you have first right to know, as I should know
To be able to come to you in case of untoward accident.

Yes, you have helped me reach this plateau of serenity
Between life and death – but while I choose life
I must pay the price for caring so much for another
Not to be swallowed up, for fear of not knowing of you.

SHE PLAYS CACHE-CACHE WITH HER LIPS
From Vilanova to Helene, who is always so charming as to be disarming, but oh, those lips that are "sweeter than wine" as the song goes, but I can only guess. May 3, 2008

("Cache-Cache," the game of hide-and-go-seek as played in French speaking countries.)

Ouuu, I got a French Canadian girl
She plays cache-cache with her lips -
One cheek here, one cheek there
Turns her head in such quick time
You'll never land one on her lips.

Ouuu, I got a French Canadian girl
She plays cache-cache with her lips -
When she talks my English lingo
Her "French" forms rosebud lips
That you're just crazy to kiss.

Ouuu, I got a French Canadian girl
She plays cache-cache with her lips -
Protecting herself, or me from what?
Becoming more than friends?
I already am, is she?

Ouuu, I got a French Canadian girl
She plays cache-cache with her lips -
Though that's a game for babies,
It spurs you on to such a degree
You're dying to land one on those lips.

Ouuu, I got a French Canadian girl
She plays cache-cache with her lips -
Whatever hidden motive she has
It's better to settle for two cheeks
Than one cheek the English way.

I KNOW, BUT THAT HELENE COULD KNOW
Vilanova May 5, 2008

You helped lift me up onto the plateau
Gave me such unstinting tenderness
That my wounds have quickly healed.
Your gift has been given and fully won,
So you could safely drift away from me
And no-one find fault at your fading image.

Now must I do battle against all who come
To win you on the plains of La Mancha
A somewhat battered Quiñones or Quixote
No more advantaged by your sympathy.

I know, but that Helene could know
What passion of spirit I have to give her
From flame-hardened crucible of heart
That pours forth the molten metal of love
Pure constancy of commitment and affection
Well-learned in the jousts with windmills
That I could never give false fealty
To one whose scarf 's knotted to my sleeve.

CELEBRATING MORE THAN MOTHER'S DAY
At at Mother's Day lunch with her sons:
These simple thoughts are my way of thanking all of you
for the great joy in feeling welcome to your private celebration.
A true family friend, Vilanova, May 11, 2008

Because we never want to be taken for granted
By someone who steps into our life
It doesn't hurt to be reminded -
For us, our children were a happening,
For them, we were always there.

Why chance a parent might only be a person
When they need a god-like cornucopia
To fill their expectations and survive.
One only graduates to person-hood
When children find their God is mortal.

So "Mother's Day" becomes underwhelming
When the boys have grown to see,
"Helene is More than Mother's Day!"
Wonderful, unique mortal and mother too!

TODAY'S GREEN FORAYS
Vilanova, with help from my daughter and friend, June 10, 2008

In my youth,
Exploring remote places,
I exulted in the unknown.
Hoping to see no one,
To find no stone trail markers,
I blazed new trails –
My raison d'etre.
The path of solitude,

Was where I sought to be
A half-century ago.

Nowadays,
Seeking well-used byways,
Shared with many hikers,
I hail each as they pass,
Hearing their kind replies,
As in a forest fugue
Of tonal variations.
My raison d'etre,
Today's green forays.

Leading me here,
With your slim hand in mine,
I bridged the stream of time.
Reaching this familiar shore,
I fulfilled my inner self
With endless love to give.

Helene knew of the well-taken fun of the two "camps" into which the de Gaia family divided to playfully joust with personality traits held by my daughter and I, called "Cheech" in contrast to those traits which gave my son and his mother, Vernique, the sobriquet of "Dormice." Basically, Dormice had a superiority complex, just short of attempting to rule Cheech, who tolerated their disdain up to the point of giving away their freedom. Dormice prided command of rational thought along with command of everything about them, while Cheech were relegated to easygoing allowances for all behavior, including eating to excess (at times.)

This poem was, therefore, composed in a sense of continuing this ritual method of poking family fun as an honorarium to Helene's friendship. Otherwise and undeniably, it's absolute silliness.

ATTENTION, HELENEMOUS
*Sighed and squealed on this broadcast by your very own Vilakins,
more graphically known as Vilemass, Le Grande Cheech*

> *Dormice,*
> *Standup on your hind paws,*
> *Never mind Cheech!*
> *Dormice,*
> *Keeping your just laws,*
> ***(and so on -- to the tune of Star Wars)***

Vernique, Late Queen Rodentia of Dormania would have rated you a 1st Class Dormouse, a caste significantly higher than us lowly Cheech who have even been known, to our final regret, to have put a good dinner before good sex. What a perversion of values.

I am only preparing you for a very serious fireside chat from yours truly, Vilamass, Le Grande Cheech, the president of Cheechillvania on our national television station reaching millions of slightly to seriously overweight cheech throughout our nation. This may cost me my next term since I am prepared to recognize the superior attributes of our neighboring Dormice from the great nation of Dormania. Response has already come: *"Now now, Head Cheech, we are not overweight - we are merely fluffly or undertall, as Vernique said in an atypical more generous (about Cheech anyway) Dormouse moment.*

In fact, I am awarding Helene, in absentia, this very evening at 7:30 pm on Channel CDL-TV -Cochon de Lait, (Laitão in Portuguesia) the Noble Peach Prize of Cheechdom, that includes an overfat violin called a Cheech-Cello, trusting you will never be impeached for playing on our national instrumentality. It is for your tireless patience, open heart (and telephone) in giving numerous additional helpings to his official Cheechness in working through his grief and maintaining his sty on the plateau. -- For your suffering through tiresome pig-outs at local eateries, enduring ballets of dancing piglets and operas dominated by the Plump-Cheech divas. As penitence, the royal weee has succumbed to Dormania, by losing 25 grossly won pounds of Cheechereeno fat-ass-ticus.

Your prize will be delivered domani to your door in Dormania on the morrow in the green Mouseratti of her deased Dormiceness of Vernicia.

BESTED BY NATURE

**Captured in Haiku by Vilanova, holding hands with Helene
in a snow-fall of cherry blossoms from my 60-ft tree.**

*Garden work pass by
Spring's cherry blossom snow
Stunned us to silence.*

While Helene and I shared so much depth of friendship during my recovery from the loss of Vernique, I soon had to accept that she was not the person that I was to "love again." Her boyfriend was coming back into the picture and my being the same age as her father added to my need to pull in my amorous reins lest I spoil our future friendship. Even as I pulled back with some natural despondence, the Gods sought to have some fun with me, seating me next to another French Canadian beauty from Montreal, also called Helene, on my next wine marketing support flight to the East Coast. Even her last name was almost the same, but she was happily married, although leaving me an invitation to visit them in Montreal.

LIZABETA: The Agony of "Dating"

Half the fun of dating Lizabeta was succumbing to the temptation to which a I hardly gave a second thought, when this friend visiting Vernique momentarily created a small spark by her saucy manner and charming dimples as I was introduced. The most affection we ever expressed was lying side-by-side, fully clothed on a large bed watching river adventure movies on a nine-foot wide projection screen at the foot of the bed while enjoying the surround sound of the watery scene. While this could have been an obvious ploy to get my dates in bed, it was also the only room large enough to handle the equipment.

FLEE TO THE WOODLAND MUSE
Musings on simple things that make a difference –
Lizabeta's Spring day was not lost to work, but inspiring that work,
as she picnics with her laptop by the river. No, I'm not making fun.
Vilanova April 24, 2008

> *Free yourself from the desk;*
> *Flee to the woodland Muse.*
> *Take your laptop with you;*
> *Paint it into Titian's scene.*
> *Never mind anachronism -*
> *Not losing a day in Spring,*
> *Inspiring every thought*
> *With the scents of nature.*

Dear Lizabeta (a letter on June 21, 2008)

Thank you for being there to continue the dialogue of life which gives insight and ultimate meaning. The film and book you loaned me to read, generates much thought, but the *Celestine Prophecy* has one major flaw that surprises me because it is so anachronistic – namely that evolution presupposes "progress" in an upward direction and even that would be different for different people. (Some of the best perspective on this fallacy can be found in the scholarly work entitled "The History of the Idea of Progress.") Evolution frequently comes to dead ends and blind alleys, often to the extinction of a species. The best thing about evolution is the frequent side effect of opening new paths (both going and coming) and freedom of thought.

I learned at a young age that I could not find my salvation through Eastern Mysticism, Protestantism, Catholicism or even Pagan Deities – but had to learn from them all and become my own person, not a hitch-hiker on someone else's ideology or concept of life. It had to be through my own tunnel of self-realization and incorporation. The most significant occurrence in my formative life as a very young man, who sometimes agonized in frustration at his inability to discover any true meaning in life, came from a mentor who simply helped me to see that the answer was already before me in the very question I asked of "the meaning of life." Understanding that it was this "meaning" in itself, with all its ramifications, a clarity entered my life that I have never lost. The frustration that was going to be beyond endurance by the time I was 30, became a capricious "black hole" that was never my nemeses.

But for your friendship, I am enchanted at what a challenging and stimulating "table" you set for your friends with all kinds of flavors and delights for the mind.

A heartfelt hug for being who you are and joy in sharing, Vilanova

DANCI: Sisterly Serenity

While recovering from the loss of Vernique, I found solace in visiting my sisters in Chicago and North Carolina, while on wine marketing support trips for distributors in those areas. I was particularly glad to have spent some quality time with my sister Danci in her North Carolina mountain home not far from Franklin, as she succumbed to already-encroaching lung cancer shortly thereafter. She had secluded herself away from too many bad male relationships in the Tampa area of Florida to be among neighbors who were more occupied with real issues of living a healthy outdoor life, than all the drama of "city folk." With her physical stamina and hearty good looks, this turned out to be a natural environment for releasing her flow of energy without getting embroiled in anything more than a brush with nature.

MY SISTER'S SMOKY MOUNTAIN SONG
Dedicated to sister Danci on Vilanova's visit, May 18, 2008

Hooray for pistol-packing girls
She's going to get our supper
At sister Danci's Mountain Home
In the Car-too-ge-chaye township
Of Springtime's velvet-cloaked Smokys.

Seeking refuge from her troubles
She made a simpler world up here
Three thousand feet above us all
In North Carolina mountains
With no computers, no cell phones.

But with a chainsaw in one hand
Oxygen bottle strapped to waist
Manages just fine on one lung
Then rests for a while in hot tub
Before trucking up to town.

No men complicating her life,
Just friends and family when needed.
Family stored far enough away
Not to create a hubbub here
Where her dog Jessie serves just fine.

No longer climbs steep forest stretch
To reach her backyard mountain crest
Though bro'Vila takes the challenge
Getting his body back in shape
For his love of wilderness walks.

Best of all when he visits her
Easy joy of brother and sister,
'Put your arms around me' kind of love
Brightening dark lonely corners
To smile again at love's hunger.

ZAFRA

Throughout my life, Zafra was always in the background, as a lifelong friend, who posed no threat to Vernique, since we all met sometimes for dinner when Vernique accompanied me on wine marketing trips to Houston.

I met Zafra at college, where she became the unrequited love that one thinks they will die over at that young age, until we met again 50 years later, following Vernique's death. Then, I discovered there had been no other suitor, stealing her love from me, only the desire to remain uncommitted until she had realized her romance with Europe, where she went to continue her studies. In fact, even her best girl friend had been unable to penetrate her emotional wall, to be able to say whether she had ever consummated a relationship.I certainly wasn't going to storm the ramparts while living in another part of the country. But I was frequently on business in her hometown.

So we had delightful dates for dinners, movies, concerts and just enjoying an easy conversation at her home. She still lived in the same home where I had picked her up for a date as a youth. Like something out of a Tennessee Williams tale of the South, but not so morbid, she casually mentioned being in the same bedroom she grew up in, not moving to the larger room of her deceased parents. When we said goodnight, there was no parting kiss. She would bend her head to my chest, so I couldn't see her face and return a tentative hug.

Yet, she said she loved me. Perhaps, it was in her mind, like her infatuation with everything written about the *Song of Solomon.* Although she could still be that "good ol' Texas gal' who wasn't afraid to casually comment to one of her girl friends that some good-looking stranger sure had a "cute butt." Vernique and Giovanna met her and understood my keeping this long friendship that kept failing to become my final love.

She died suddenly on January 19, 2014, of an unidentified brain tumor, shortly after I met Terra. With my new involvement, and giving up hope of a closer relationship, I had not talked to Zafra in one of our weekly phone conversations after Giovanna's death for several months. Only one East Coast relative knew of our timeless love or friendship that had maintained itself through my two wives, whom it never threatened. She called to tell me what happened, but there was no time to go to the funeral. This was not a good closure to losing someone I had loved almost all of my life.

A TRUER LOVE I WILL NEVER KNOW
Vilanova to Zafra, June 23, 2008

A truer love I will never know, than Zafra.
She gives herself not to me, but to all of life.
Now I see why she waved aside my young ardor
More than fifty years ago –
Voyaging to sate her longing for the old world,
Not to break the cadence of her evolution
That plays its symphony across her face,
Gently touched by all the years of passage.

Her great charm lies within her cosmic being -
Within never faltering sense of purpose
To explore life's surrounding songs.
For two evenings she sang to me of life's voyage,
Like a thousand and one of Scheherazade,
Drawing out my joyous response –
Closing the circle of pilgrimage
From the source of youthful ardor.

Finding her, no longer cloaked by my lust,
I delight in the radiance of her thoughts.
Within the cradle of her heart
Lies a deep, yet wary affection for me

That shares an element of touching warmth,
Celebrating the passions of our minds.
Walking hand-in-hand among the live oaks
We join together all fifty years in between.

WHO SITS BY THE STREAM, OBSERVING
To Zafra from Vianova, Oct 2012

Ne'er loneliness that drives us together,
But undemanding joy in each other
Budding from lusts and cautions of youth
Into a life-long twining that gives
An ease to every shared moment.

"Como solo amarte mi amor pretendio,
Solo de quererte pagado estoy."
(My heart only wanted to love you,
And in loving you, I am already satisfied.)
Cantata con voce sola, Handel

Realizing so much in another life,
You earned the right to sit by the stream
Observing well the plight of us all -
So engulfed in the torrent of life
That we often learn only too late,
Ignoring your very sage advice –
Not seeing how you could know so much.

JOCELYN

"Taking off my jacket, belt and shoes is almost like beginning to undress in public," I commented to the tall blonde with long, flowing flaxen hair, as we prepared to go through the x-ray security at the airport. I couldn't help but notice her toe comically protruding through a run in her stocking, as I inanely sought an introduction. Her otherwise meticulous attire and grooming was in such sharp contrast that I wanted to caress the offending toe, although she chose to be totally indifferent, not to draw attention to it.

Getting on the plane together, she was surprised, as much as I was at my own folly, when I suddenly appeared, easing down into the open first class seat beside her. With a bit of fiction about "my long lost girl friend," I had convinced the flight attendant to move me up to travel with Jocelyn from forlorn exile in the coach section.

SILENT AFFIRMATION OF HIS FAITH

Vilanova to Jocelyn, before he too is thrust into the Maelstrom, June 20, 2008

When he cautioned her not to join the hike,
She saw he could respect the total focus
Her work demanded at this crucial point.

He slipped once or twice - a soft intrusion,
But without reply had the trust and confidence
To keep cheering onward with divertissement
Hoping only with light diversion to give some joy.
It mattered not whether she read them at the time,
Non-intrusive, but consistent as a warm embrace
That confirmed her silent affirmation of his faith.

Relative, of course,
To all the intensity which I project,
I make light of how strongly I feel –
Not to weigh you down with it all.

We only met four days before,
Yet the last week apart from you
Spins our short time into a web
That captures all the best moments
Of our lifetime,
(If I may boldy speak for you.)

Like two harmonic chords
Streaming through the sky
We heard each other's sigh,
Met and melded,
But still as two.

TO JOCELYN, A JOCELYN
Vilanova to Jocelyn, June 29, 2008 . . . of Cavafy's great poem

Ci siamo trovati nel corridoio di tempo
E sono diventato immediatamente gli amici.
*"We found each other in the corridor of time
And became friends immediately."
- translated from Guiseppi Leafoli's poem "A Virgine"*

Do not fear the strain of the voyage
Will leave this love in its wake
For our hearts are lashed together
At the helm of our driven craft.

Docking side-by-side at exotic ports
We share moments of grand adventure,
Exploring the coast of each other
Per chance to reach the inner self,
At the well of all our travels.

ITHACA *(excerpts)*
Constantine P. Cavafy (1911)

> *". . . Ithaca has given you the beautiful voyage.*
> *She has nothing more to give you.*
> *Wise as you have become, with so much experience,*
> *you must already have understood what Ithacas mean."*

To Jocelyn, Vernique has left you a much better Vilanova: Probably the biggest thorn in our long and successful marriage was having two independent and intelligent people who had rather low tolerance levels for errors or omissions. It took me years not to just suppress but to expunge what Vernique called my "ill-concealed rage." Never abusive, but damaging enough to send me to the rose garden for penitent sleep the next night or two.

I particularly hated to be presumed at fault. Whether I was at fault or not, decided itself as I was quick to cast the blame, until I learned that blame never solved any problem, but only made it worse.

Travel is often the best test of a relationship. When couples are removed from their supporting environment and retreats, they have to deal with all their interpersonal relationships head on. Vernique was always my navigator while traveling by car in foreign countries. But she was smart enough to simply throw the map at me when we would get lost and I would blame her. So in the frustration of being lost and in fear of fault myself, I became most definitely at fault for casting blame where it didn't matter, when we only needed "to turn the page" to find our way to where ever we were going. Of course, Vernique too had her own "little devils" inside that she had to expunge in realizing an increasingly deep relationship.

I am sharing so many details of my life with you because I am optimistic enough to think that God or whatever fates will allow me to once more share, perhaps, an even more mature love, after all I have learned, and continue to learn about making the most out of every moment that life has to offer. Otherwise, I am perfectly happy to be by myself with friends and family.

Cherishing all we are finding in each other, Vilanova

A TORRENT, YES – BUT IN NO HURRY
TO EXPLORE THE SHORES OF YOUR BEING
Vilanova to Jocelyn, July 2008

I cannot escape looking you in the eye
You stand out in the crowd of passers by
With a fluid serenity as you walk along
Making your way through the throng
To where our two heads meet above them all.

Almost intimidating in your sure composure,
Yet touchingly vulnerable with a run at the toe
Of your stocking foot freed from your boot
To pass through the airport inspection.

Your wide smile framed by a cascade of hair,
Neither inviting or aloof, but surviving with humor
All that business travel throws in our way.
I felt an unbridled attraction to know you
That trampled over any reticence.

Not looking to meet anyone while en-route,
Some kindred cord brought us to wait together
To test the waters with a bit of inner selves,
That soon confirmed our inexorable impulse.

Little did you suspect to unleash a waterfall
Built up by so many years of focused attention
That it came at you as an intense torrent --
Wanting only to give you joy, not taking
But leaving you feeling a need to respond
Without room to turn in the confines of business.

But now you must know that while it's a torrent
There's no hurry to explore the shores of your being,
Only to let you know that it flows along your stream
With a refreshing constancy to what ever challenges,
To always be there for you without fear of losing it,
Having glimpsed straight into the eye of your soul.

Dearest Jocelyn, (*from Vilanova to Jocelyn, July 4, 2008, while she is at the family reunion*)

Perhaps, you expect too much fealty from love. To "worship" you might mean that you would have to spend a lot of time on a pedestal, when I would rather simply adore you by my side. I have always told my friends to desist being match-makers, that if I was to meet that "adorable woman," it would have to be in the stream of my life.

Good things continue to happen to me with such astonishing regularity that I am beginning to believe in good fairies (the straight kind). For why would some transcendent being or force bother to take notice of this one of billions of humans? Perhaps, because – despite all horrors that are perpetrated by mankind as the worst of all predators – I steadfastly believe that some cosmic morality is embedded in this human game plan.

Yes, "good happenings," because you are certainly "Celeste Jocelyn," meeting the way we did. You have high expectations of those you might love, but tempered with compassion and steadfast good faith in the potential of one whom you gave access to your path. My entire being rejoiced in our verbal paseo this evening. I feared that I might have lost the chance to reach your heart when I failed to end a delightful movie evening with a toast to just the two us. At least I was there (in spirit) with your story of when, as a child, you took the pin off your pocket and your mom reach in only to discover a mouse. I did a similar thing at age six letting loose several pet white mice that completely disrupted my Aunt Emily's ladies garden party in Corpus Christi, Texas.

The "up-side" of our recent personal challenge proves that our relationship has the capability of working through things in a positive way that brings us even closer. Since we are so in tune with each other that we were both simultaneously well aware of the problem before it was confronted, there was easy resolution – which speaks well for working through any future challenges.

I want to add a meaningful, joyous element to your life that fits whatever is important to you. Through difficult times of any type, I have proven to myself and friends that I am the bulwark you seek, and that two self-sufficient people dedicated to each other can make the daily colors of life just that much brighter.

What a delight to adore you, Vilanova

REALIZING THE GIFT
OF THE GREAT JOURNEY
From Vilanova to Jocelyn, August 3, 2008

Curiosity is the hallmark of our two beings,
Exploring all that is wonderfully unique
In each other,
In our world,
All about us.

We always revel in seeing for the first time
The true essence of every wondrous variation
In each other,
In our world,
All about us.

We opened the path to our innermost selves,
A chance to experience a totally new love
In each other,
In our world,
Mind in mind.

Realizing the gift of the great journey together,
I hope not too late to love you for your self,
If it is to be
With each other,
Heart to heart.

To my very dear friend, Jocelyn: While life can never be put into a box so it is easy to manage, I have been trying to get a better understanding of the parameters and factors influencing our unique relationship. The first step was to further explore the meaning of "friendship". Sometimes I think I am like a dog -- worrying a bone to death and, perhaps, entangling us in too much thinking. You are becoming such an integral part of my rebirth that I know that you will see the positive direction of this dialogue and want to participate.

Most definitions of friendship recognize "that it involves some degree of intimacy" which I am missing in our relationship. We can be very organized and seem to navigate a bit of life's voyages in our minds, but often run aground on the shoals and rocks of emotions that seem to ebb and flow at nature's whim.

with all my mind and heart, Vilanova –

Back to my original decision to give up dating . . . I had already come to the realization that she was "enslaved" to her Korean boss through fear of losing her high-level electronics sales job. His demands cancelled many of our weekend plans, as noted in this ditty:

KEEP YOUR KOREANS
from Vilanova to Jocelyn, Aug 19, 2008

Keep your Koreans and their Taekwondo;
I'll take my Kenyans and their Ho Jambo!

Thanks for the voyage in your busy life,
For saving my heart from the surgeon's knife.

I'll always adore, – even worship you,
For Verity, Brilliance and Beauty too.

For warning that we can only be friends
When October's leaves color the glens.

Reminding myself that I had been "fulfilled" with Vernique, - that I didn't need to agonize over Jocelyn, I have the option to say to hell with all the drama of dating, I will depend on occasionally visiting with friends and family for the amount of time they can stand me, and forego the conjugal bed. Don't believe it! I leave the door open just a crack in case I might be "oh so lucky," which, indeed, I am. The door soon swings open to find myself marrying an "Amazonian Athlete," Giovanni, who's 20-years younger than me. She has excelled in every sport from professional skiing to riding and fly fishing – casting 90 feet onto the target fish.

The shout of "fish-on" scares my friends and family almost as much as the jolt from our quick marriage to her two daughters in their twenties. But I'm not surprised at such a quick catch. I don't have time this near the end of life to laboriously ponder decisions that I feel sure to recognize as the right thing from life's experience.

Like the gambler who endows the slot machine with compassion for how much he has already invested in the random spins of fate, the wheel spins again displaying indifference by taking my all for nothing. In less than two years of bliss, I am almost destroyed by her sudden slip into addiction that comes from a growing tolerance to sports pain-management drugs. Needing more and more pain-killers, she adds alcohol to fill-in as drugs become less effective. Our life together becomes an increasing nightmare, until an accidental mix of two conflicting prescription drugs creates an overdose, cutting her life short at age 57 after only four years together.

CHAPTER NINE – LOVING AGAIN, A SELF-DESTRUCT

GIOVANNA

After some time, when I had given up all hope of ever "loving again," and being satisfied that I had already had a magnificent fulfillment, I met Giovanna on a blind date to the ballet and found the courage to realize that I had found my "soul mate." Best of all, it was reciprocal. Like me, she had almost closed the door, deciding to become content with family and friends, so both of us were surprised to find each other in the normal course of our lives. From then on, our commitment and marriage happened so fast that it left everyone around us in shock.

When we met for the first date, she was fresh from the shower, wrapped in a bath towel with another creating a turban for her wet hair, making her taller than my 6'2" height. Her forthright nature immediately became apparent as she laughed at my being early, while she proved to be habitually late and stressed at being rushed. She carried her sinewy body like an athletic fashion model. Temporarily working as a caretaker of a dying, elderly woman, the anguish had caused her to lose so much weight that her stockings started falling down while in the car. I dubbed her *"Falling Down Stocking"* in the American Indian nickname vernacular.

There was no tell-tale premonition to the twist of fate that was to come. Giovanna's slide into drug and alcohol addiction mocked the very premise of "love again before the end of time." It threw me into such a deep hopelessness and depression that the end of time almost superseded love.

THE PERFECT BEGINNING, A COURAGEOUS ENCOUNTER
Vilanova to Giovanna, November 8, 2008

We should all meet each other fresh from the shower,
Sans artifice, clothed only in the petals of our flower
In a pure white robe that alters nothing of who we are.
What a beginning. The courage to lay yourself bare
In a new encounter, to be as you are, like it or leave it.

She had not intended to greet me in this fashion.
But not abashed at being caught in her ablution,
She set events in motion that laid bare the petals
To the inner stamen of our lives and thoughts.
The perfect beginning. The courage to be transparent
To fall into perfect step together, as knowing forever.

The melody of our encounter was in total harmony
With the ballet of New Works, with non nobis, domine,*
Even to leaving when it became discordant.
Neither expected to repeat the "one great love"
That plays the vital theme in whom we have become,
But, perchance to share a lingering finish to our wine
Which honors and refreshes when our lives en-twine.

*non nobis, domine, "gift of thanksgiving and humility"
PS: *"Life on its own terms is worth living. - The ultimate*
justification of the work of art is to help the spectator to
become a work of art himself." – Bernard Berenson

THE ADVENTURESS
To Giovanna from Vilanova, while flying to Texas – Nov 15, 2008

To love again before the end of time –
Worrying our bodies in the lion's jaws,
Tempering thrusting thighs in thermal springs,
(The ad advises: It's not for the weak of heart.)
But seeing the wind blowing to the far horizon,
The Adventuress and I unfurl our top-gallants,
To smash through the froth of breaking seas,
Cleaving the waves that climax life's passions,
Stretching the fabric of our fragile-skin vessels
To the point of no return on love-racked bodies.

FAR AWAY BUT, OH SO NEAR
YOU DEFINE AND DELIGHT
ALL OF MY SENSES
Giovanna from Vilanova, December 14, 2008 Kenya

*Right after marrying Giovanna I left for Africa, continuing a
charitable project.. We went together the next year.*

*In the clear air of the Kenyan Mara,
I inhale the natural scent of your body.
Entranced by the sleek-bodied cheetah,
I am wrapped in your own strong thighs.*

*The early morning birdsong of the bush,
Captures your laughter's sweet falsetto.
The mating grunts and growls of lions
Raise the phoenix of our own passion.*

*The African sun warms me to the quick,
Feeling myself in the hearth of your body.
The trusting gaze of the Kenyan children,
Lifts my soul in your pure, unreserved love.*

*In the wild taste of primal African food,
I savor every part of your unique being.
In every moment of every day away,
Oh so far, but - oh so near,
You define and delight all of my senses.*

Before going to Italy with Giovanna in April: Although she
worked for 12 years as a flight attendant on Alaska Airlines for part
of her career, she had never been to Europe, only Russia. So I
wanted to give her a very special time in April, 2009. A former
professional athlete, who was one of eight women on a US K2
Women's Ski Team in the seventies, Giovanna helped develop the
women's clothing section at a major national sporting goods store,

and was an action model for several clothing and ski equipment manufacturers. She rounded up cattle from horseback on cattle drives. She wore very little make-up, no perfume and abhorred pretentiousness. Her mind was open to all the beautiful things in the world, especially interaction with people of different interests and nationalities. Music flowed through her veins, and she was once a very fine oboe player.

You can see my challenge, finding the right balance of things to do over a few weeks for a woman who would be as happy staying at a remote farm as a castle, yet who loved music and museums. We were aware of a national holiday in Italy during our short visit. So, while Giovanna prefered spontaneity, being open to adventure, we did have to make some general plans, which included staying at one of my wine producer's castle, box seats for a ballet at La Scala in Milan, and fantastic dining after a private viewing of art treasures.

THE TORPOR OF FULFILLMENT
Vilanova, July 2, 2009

Being fulfilled again with Giovanna
My pen doesn't spend itself on paper.
I cannot claim poetry as my trade
Creating little marvels through discipline.
My pen only seems to flow from passion,
Drawing a pathway beyond oblivion,
Exploring the rare corners of this life.
Satiated, my pen has come to rest,
Only to scroll again through some torment
Or to explain this torpor - fulfillment.

THE PALE MORNING BLUE DUN
Vilanova to Giovanna, Aug 2, 2009

Casting a "Blue Dun"fly at Purgatory, Cascade Creek, Colorado.
Giovanna taught me the rudiments of fly fishing, that I put to test in
Colorado over a weekend escape during a business trip.

> *You gave me this joy on the mountain creek*
> *In the cool morning of my creek-side watch*
> *The fly line unfurls as pale morning Blue Dun*
> *Hits the surface of a placid backwater*
> *Under the tree trunk spanning the creek banks*
> *Below the crashing of the boulder falls*
> *The trout takes the dun, thanks Giovanna -*
> *You weave your magic even from afar.*

Working through desperate moments: As in all relationships,
there are moments we have to work through, words said that we
wish we could push back in time so they never happened. Working
through desperate moments can often strengthen the bond of love.
All my friends who claimed to have never argued or had to work
through challenging moments with their spouse have ended in
broken relationships. I almost missed the chance to work through
my ill-placed sharp words, having nearly died of a pulmonary
embolism caused by having four hernias repaired by surgery at the
same time only a month before. Giovanna's flight attendant training
contributed significantly to saving my life, after I fell to the tiled
floor at 4 a.m. one morning, getting ready to leave on a business trip.

WORLD WITHOUT END, AMEN
Vilanova to Giovanna Oct 15, 2009

> *I thought I could lift myself above,*
> *Being my own worst enemy,*
> *Robbing myself and Giovanna*
> *Of the perfect love for each other.*
> *Breaking the magical spell*
> *With another petty verbal slam.*

The bitter cycle played out again.

Had I died on Monday as near I did,
My memory would have been revered
Through all the river of tears and loss.
But she saved my life,
Though it is now empty
Since I played what may be my final turn
Of the bitter cycle of hurt.

Worse than death the anguish I leave her,
Bitter loss, as all those loves corrupted
Thursday's death knell of love's trust,
For Giovanna can only endure so much.

Could I expect her to lay heart open again?
Am I doomed to be chained to the wall
Of myself, my own worst enemy
For the rest of my life?
Is there no redemption?
Only World without end, amen?

To Giovanna – October 2009   Last night I slept but little, but wormed my way through the valley of the shadow of myself – to seek some renewal, to shed some tired skins, to gain release from some shackles of the unconscious self – for myself and for you. You, whom I love and respect more than life itself. Your constant love that enabled me to love and all the better to respect myself as the object of your love.

Yes, it is so unfair that you should suffer even a moment of "ill-concealed rage." You had nothing to do with it. It was born of rejection, of developing total self-reliance in the face of being very much alone in dealing with authority as a child and adolescent – because this "authority" never understood but always threatened, like being on a raging sea in a small boat with only myself to carry through. Then, you came and I was no longer alone. The rage has diminished, but needs to have its remnants rooted out, needs to have no excuse to continue, especially with the chance of you being caught up in its warpath. You are never the cause, only the victim who got trampled by the berserk elephant.

I never could tolerate an "Oh, Henry!"- as a resigned stepmother exclaimed to my father turning aside and going ahead with the day in resignation rather than confrontation. I don't want this kind of relationship any more than you would stoop to tolerate, to condone the ugly part of my nature. Much better that I work my way through this tunnel, go to the depths of darkness and return with less baggage.

To be touched by your life is the great joy of your friends and acquaintances. To share your life is a god-given privilege that I truly appreciate --- so I have a special obligation to myself, god and you to finally shed this old skin and give you fair return, a fairer balance in our life together. And how refreshing it is, even after a long and wrenching night to show that one is never too old, too ingrained, to raise one's self from the mire of unconscious behavior. Not to have to control bad behavior but to grow beyond it. Proving a lizard might grow a new head as well as a tail.

GIOVANNA SEARCHES FOR SABILA - (Aloe Vera)
By Vilanova - Cancun June 5, 2010, Saturday evening

Two days on the beach, even with care
Sunburn attacks my shoulders and back.
Giovanna gets hotel gardener
To cut fresh Sabila cactus tips,
From which she squeezes the inner gel
Across the flaming parts of my skin.

How much better nature's remedy
Than store-bought plastic tubes.of ointment.
Even better Giovanna's searching
For the local Sabila cactus,
Despite the concierge saying that –
"There are no such plants growing 'round here.

She presses on and gets the barman
Committed to her relentless cause.
To alert gardener to her need –

Who gladly delights to demonstrate
His very ancient Mayan knowledge
Of medicinal plants that grow here.

So ends the loving tale of my love's
Winning search for the Sabila sauve
That takes the pain from burning skin
While warming the core of my heart.

DAYS OF QUIET STROKING
Vilanova to Giovanna June 15, 2010

These days of quiet stroking
Lying side-by-side in bed
Our serenity unchallenged
Even the rain gods can't foul
The warmth of our entwined selves.

Yet, should some tempest blow in,
Though no cause should give it rise,
You might wrap in your travel cloak,
Sojourn in some desert,
Sorting ill winds from yourself
'Til you ride the guiding star
On that trail of trust's return.

By a hoof-beat, bringing self back
Though not forgetting the slight
So uncalled for under any -
Wasted anger, foolish hurt –
Not due to you but blind thought.
Rejoice in quiet stroking.

FOREWARNING SPURNED: Vernique's closest friend, Babalu, and her husband had tried to warn me about what some associate had confided to them concerning Giovanna. But these were the same friends who just shortly before had recommend Giovanna for my blind date meeting and who later became witnesses to our wedding and joined in the following celebration. With all of my early passionate intensity in full swing and very strong feelings about loyalty in my commitment, I stared them down and refused to hear any gossip, after which I kept them at arms length until the end and healing.

IT SLIPPED BEYOND MY GRASP

Vilanova, November 2010 After working through my own foibles, the furies dropped down on me with all the swirling tempest that addiction can spin up into a tornado of devastation.

To love again before the end of time
To find the person, not just fill the void
Of aging loneliness
To share the gift of the one I left behind
The richness, apex of a life fulfilled
Love without end, amen

Too anxious to soar beyond the furies
To soon my love betrayed my trust
Lost in her addictions
No time for me to play it out again
Nor even weather our dissolution
The end of time is here.

Perhaps, I will just endure the remnants
Of the love sought before the end of time.
Not able to endure
The wasteland in trials of separation
Let the furies be the victor of my fate
Love's coward at the end.

COMING UP FOR AIR
FROM THE KITTY LITTER BOX
Vilanova December 12, 2011

Sometimes, there's tragi-comedy to addiction
Falling bare-assed into the kitty litter box
Bleary eyes staring up from the bathroom floor
Again and again, like you wanted to die
Tempted to let you, but call 911 as ever
Kindly paramedics have become like family
This time I'm told not to take you home,
"So you see the consequences of your actions."

Hospital will dump you on the night-time streets
Desperate you call all your drinking friends
But I have forewarned them not to enable
Only, I can't leave you to the cold streets,
Agree to pick you up in the morning
Our marriage almost wrecked on this reef.

Depression as I have never known
Just managing day-by-day as we drown.
Then, somehow from the depths of oblivion
Comes your gasp for air, for struggling up
To the shimmering light at the water's surface

Inpatient recovery for addiction lasts 21 days.
At point of "I can't take any more", you give hope.
As the month passes, you become better
Passing beyond those desperate days.

Not to be the ultimate enabler, I finally sum up the courage to draw a line in the sand which cannot be crossed by Giovanna without exceeding the limits that I am willing to endure.

To Giovanna, a preface to an agreement for continuing our marriage: Revised Dec 13, 2011

I love the true Giovanna and am proud and happy for your interaction, courage and progress at the Recovery Center, but I am too conditioned from the holocaust of the last two years to trust in the future. That you are rising like Excalibur from the depths of addiction and a zombie-like existence is wonderful, but there is a long and challenging road ahead where you will have to battle with King County, attorneys, legal impositions on your time and activities for up to the next five years.

The recent DUI accidents could have led to costly lawsuits and damages beyond our insurance that could have used up all my retirement assets. In the three years we have been married, you have contributed virtually nothing material to our resources, only growing financial burden, depletion of my limited retirement funds, and damage to some of my business relationships.

Time and again I have been infatuated by the momentary rapture of the clearing of the sky when you awake like sleeping beauty to seduce me into continuing and then falling back into the growing nightmare of living with an alcoholic and drug addict.

If your reaction is to slip back into addiction, or to become a recluse from normal social and family activities, or expect me to carry your burden, I will not and cannot do it without destroying myself. I know that you love me, so you will want me to protect my well-being in the relatively short time I have in the balance of my life, compared to your potential 20 more years than I have.

Likewise, I don't think you want me to have to spend all my time focusing on these problems that you have brought on yourself and that you need to have the courage to resolve without dragging my life into it on a never ending day-to-day downward spiral. Your love obligates you to save the ones you love and get them off this belt line to the grave.

Therefore, I ask you to sign the attached agreement – this line in the sand beyond which things cannot go - so that I can continue our marriage without fear of losing my health and retirement resources.

Your loving and long-supportive husband, Vilanova

Agreement for Continuing our Marriage

Revised December13, 2011 to respond to Giovanna and staff concerns after presentation on the day of consultation at Valley General Hospital Recovery Center on December 5, 2011,

My husband Vilanova de Gaia advised me, Giovanna de Gaia, that he has reached his final level of tolerance for my behavior and cannot continue our marriage if I revert to the any of the same behavior patterns upon completing my first stage of recovery as an inpatient of the recovery center. If I wish to return home with him on Dec. 16th, I agree to give him an uncontested divorce should I repeat any of the following previous behavior that he can no longer tolerate:

- Zero tolerance for alcoholic beverage consumption or excessive drugs
- Seek marriage counseling
- Mental abuse that is excessive and caused by continued addiction
- Financial depletion of retirement capital, through un-necessary legal, medical, car damage and general mishandling of funds, loss of glasses, etc
- Total dependency on him to take care of all aspects of my existence while I spend most of the day in a fog of addiction in bed , excepting normal illness, surgery, etc.
- Disruption of his business at home or on business trips with him by medical emergencies caused by excessive alcohol consumption

- Two recent DUI arrests
- The lack of active companionship where I merely allow myself to exist without rational, normal social interaction. This has also curtailed any real social life
- Continued lies and misconduct so that he can no longer trust me
- Requiring him to spend almost all of his free time being a care taker for my largely self-inflicted health problems
- Failure to follow through with outpatient addiction recovery through regular active involvement in AA meetings, psychiatric help, and normal management of my own life
- Failure to deal with and manage the financial and legal ramifications of my DUI arrests

I understand that if he needs to file for an uncontested divorce, he will continue to assist me with basic maintenance in addition to my use of my own disability funds to the extent of reasonable shelter and sustenance, including health insurance for the period of one year.

Vilanova understands that all of the above tolerance limits are subject to a degree of reasonable behavioral flexibility that would be expected of any person without addiction with the exception of alcoholic consumption that has a zero tolerance.

Signed by Giovanna de Gaia_____Dec. 13, 2011

Vilanova de Gaia _____ Dec 13, 2011

Witnessed by _____ Dec 13, 2011

Please print name_____

WAR HEROES & ATHLETIC HEROES: While Giovanna spends 21 days of inpatient rehabilitation, I prepare a status and summary of conditions and her addiction recovery as of December 26, 2011

SOCIETY FAILS TO REINTEGRATE OUR YOUTH, DAMAGED IN GIVING THEIR BEST TO OUR COUNTRY

Just as our society sometimes fails to assist the needs of returning servicemen and women to help them overcome severe Post Traumatic Stress Disorder (PTSD) and other psychological and physiological damages of war that threaten normal behavioral reintegration to society, so do we have little understanding of the needs of our top athletes to which we give so much admiration for their performance on the field and so little help in their recovery from lifelong injuries and pain management.

As one of the eight women on one of the renowned K-2 Ski Teams, and a professional ski instructor at Sun Valley, Idaho; an early innovator for combining ballet movements on the ski slopes, and a multiple award winning equestrian, Giovanna entertained and taught a wide audience throughout the nation. But sports injuries to her spine, knee and wrists, resulted in receiving early medicare disability in her fifties, not without having to spend $5,500 on an attorney to prove her need. She then obtained help from the Pain Management clinic at Virginia Mason Hospital in Seattle.

Professional Pain Management Leads to Addiction –
NOT Recreational Addiction

As her body built up tolerance to each type of pain medicine, such as methadone and oxycodone, she had to take higher and higher dosages, until it got to the point of addiction and she was abruptly cut off all drugs with seemingly nowhere to go but slide into alcoholic addiction, where she again built up tolerances and needed more and more to manage her pain.

Failure to Assess Contributing Psychological Causes –
Giovanna Begins Recovery Program

Until the psychiatrist for the Hospital Behavioral Health section conducted a Psychiatric Assessment of Giovanna in late November of 2011, when she was a voluntary in-patient, she had little support for alleviating the contributing symptoms to addiction of Chronic Depression (Dysthymia) , Post-Traumatic Stress Disorder (PTSD) and Bi-Polar Disorder. Improvement in her recovery chances for addiction was almost immediately noticeable as her psychiatric needs were medicated. After her addiction recovery, Giovanna also received psychiatric help in dealing with severe sexual child abuse by her step-father.

Giovanna Commits to Continuing Addiction Recovery:
At this stage, Giovanna was able to fully recognize her need to commit to long-term in-patient and out-patient recovery. She went into the 21-day inpatient program at a Hospital Addiction Recovery Center. At the same time, she learned to take full responsibility for her behavior and its consequences. Completing the in-patient program on Dec. 16, 2011, she started attending daily AA meetings until she could start the long-term IOP (Intensive Out-patient Program), beginning just after Christmas 2011. This program involved three days a week of three hour sessions that continued for one to two months as needed. Giovanna began learning to deal with her pain and psychological issues, completely free of alcohol or drugs since the treatment began in November at Overlake Hospital in Bellevue, Washington.

Failure of Medicare-Based Insurance to Cover In-Patient Addiction Recovery:
Many elderly and disabled people suffering substance addiction are denied economic access to in-patient treatment because Medicare does not cover addiction recovery even with supplemental insurance. We know of only one local facility in Lacey, Washington, providing coverage, with a long waiting list and often a distant drive for visiting family support necessary to evolving stages of recovery and following Intensive Out-Patient care. Giovanna's recovery has cost more than $25,000 in recent months.

More important than funding her recovery, I supported it with full participation, while giving her breathing room for working things out in group sessions where I might have inhibited her interaction. After seeking assistance from Alanon, I found that I achieved more understanding of her problems by periodically joining her at AA meetings, where I got a more positive understanding of addiction than Alanon's somewhat adversarial response. This resulted in the following eulogy to AA (Alcoholics Anonymous) that I presented at a meeting.

FINDING HUMANITY
From Vilanova to AA friends in North Bend, WA, March 2012

To share with you
Who embraced us –
This eulogy
To rebirth.
You shared with us
Your humility –
The serenity
Of open arms
That saved me
And my wife.
You shared with us
Where you've been,
What's become
Your only way
Of living on
Safe from torment.
Now it speaks
To all of us,
Since we became
One of you
In harmony.
Joining in
This legacy
Of humanity,
This releasing force
Which constantly
Regenerates
Through AA
Fellowship.

FREE OF ADDICTION, NOT LIFE
Vilanova, - upon Giovanna's death August 25, 2012

Know the truth and it shall set you free
Emblazoned above the columned entry
And the brow that adorns your mind.

Delighting in Bill Moyer's revelation in
"The Hijacked Brain" video
You wanted to share this discovery
With all who fought their addiction.

But knowing the truth you felt free
To play cat'n'mouse with your life
With pills and wine you thought
Could still be a part of the experiment.

Dulling the edges of pain and torment,
You slipped past the edge of control
Into a deathly sleep and left our world.

ODE TO GIOVANNA
Vilanova, Raleigh-Durham Airport, September 18, 2012

Trying to focus on all the joy of our life together,
I am overwhelmed with desolation of the crowds
An indifferent stream sweeping through the airport
Where I am isolated in the flow of humanity.
Absolutely alone with my grief at losing you.

Death from accidental prescription overdose follows a shoulder operation.

"Obituary: With her long blond hair swirling about her face as her six-foot tall, silk-like passage swirled through 360's, Giovanna d'Gaia was the first Sun Valley Resort ski instructor to teach ballet-freestyle on old Baldy in the mid-1970's. Surviving many ski injuries during her career, it is ironic that Giovanna d'Gaia, 57, of North Bend, Washington died Saturday, Aug. 25, from an accidental drug overdose following surgery for a fly fishing accident. She broke her left shoulder on the Snoqualmie River rocks fronting her home. She was a noted fly fishing instructor and helped Orvis Sporting Good develop their national line of women's sporting equipment and clothing while on the staff at the Vermont headquarters."

Giovanna's pioneering in Ski Ballet has not been a part of competitive freestyle skiing for some time, and was later renamed Acroski, becoming a third freestyle discipline. From late-1960s until 2000, it was performed on smooth slopes as a program of flips, jumps, rolls, leg crossings, and spins. During Giovanna's years at Sun Valley in the the mid-1970s, the routine was often done to music. Featured in the 1988 and 1992 Winter Olympics, it has since diminished in popularity with the International Ski Federation ceasing all competition after 2000.

A SUN VALLEY SONG

This skier's parody of "The Cowboy's Lament," an appropriate memorial for Giovanna as a well-known ski instructor for Sun Valley Lodge in the seventies.

The following text is from the Indiana University Folklore Archives by a student who learned it from a roommate at the University of Denver in 1950.

> *When I was a-skiing the hills of Sun Valley,*
> *As I was a-skiing old Baldy one day,*
> *I spied a young skier all wrapped in Alpaca*
> *All wrapped in alpaca, and cold as der Schnee. (snow)*
> *I see by your suntan that you are a skier,*
> *These words he did say as I boldly schussed by;*
> *Come fall down beside me and hear my sad story,*

I caught a right edge and I'm dying today.

It was once upon Baldy I used to ski gaily,
It was once upon Baldy I used to ski by;
It was first down the canyon, and then through the
narrows,
I caught a right edge and I know I must die.

Get six from the ski school to carry my coffin,
Get six little bunnies to sing me a song;
Oh lower me gently and sprinkle Schnee o'er me,
For I was a skier, my life was not long.

What killed my wife Giovanna on Aug 25, 2012, after a successful operation?

Answer to internet search of drugs involved: *"Oxycontin and clonazepam taken together are VERY DEADLY."*

The mixture of these two prescription medications were given to Giovanna by two doctors from separate clinics, who evidently were not thorough in reviewing her list of current meds. –

Internet "Best Answer:"

"Heath Ledger died recently because he mixed a pain killer, an antidepressant, and an anti-anxiety agent, by doctor's orders in therapeutic doses, not as a recreational drug to get high. Klonopin is an anti-anxiety agent and oxycodone is a pain killer so that's 2/3."

"On April 15, 2010, I lost this wonderful, intelligent and forever loving son. He was only 28 years old. He has been dealing with neck, head and shoulder pain for many years and after many other narcotics were tried and he got addicted to them, he went through the Narcotics Anonymous program and got off all the medications, except an anti-inflammatory, dicloflenac. He was in pain daily but no tests could identify what the problem was."

"MRI's, CAT's, blood work-ups, rheumatologist, neurologist, bone specialists, physical therapy could not find the cause of his

headaches and pain which turned his ears, neck and shoulders from a light red to maroon coloring. His pain was so unbearable and he went to the doctor (of which he had signed for them to NOT prescribe ANY medications without going through me, his mom, first and they prescribed clonazepam to him without my knowledge ".

"The hospital staff, doctors, funeral home and the cemetery all told us they are seeing a lot of this type of death. Almost daily, they are trying to save someone who has taken this combo and the hospital staff said they had NEVER SEEN ANYONE SURVIVE this."

APURAR CIELOS PRETENDO . . .*
Vilanova, September 19, 2012 after Giovanna's death on August 25th

Shaking my fist at an empty sky
Recalling how she cared for me –
It is such a terrible irony
That I should live to be without her
Despite my twenty more years of age.

Trying to give so deeply of herself
But how seldom giving to herself.
Fearful that it would not be enough,
She often succumbed to oblivion
Cloaking her gift in a nightmare.

She threw away life so casually
Without even knowing she was going.
Surviving all her skiing injuries,
She died trying to fool addiction
With "just another"swallow of pills.

*The title is from Pedro Calderón de la Barca's famous play **La Vida Es Sueno (Life is a Dream)** – "**Apurar, cielos, pretendo,** ya que tratais así, qué delito cometí contra vosotros naciendo:" Segismundo famous soliloquy "in which he complains to Heaven for being deprived of his liberty."

WHERE HAVE ALL THE FLOWERS GONE?
Vilanova, San Antonio, September 29, 2012

Where have all the flowers gone,
Long time passing.
Where have Vernique and G'vanna gone,
Short time passing.
Their unseen hands still grasping
At the film-like flicker of my life –

A tender drag on the moving shadows
Of what is passing by and left to be.
I am ever grateful that two women
Of such different passions
Gave their deepest love to me.

"Each person is different, has different passions and different loves, both Vernique and Giovanna had you." – Armando Serena, upon Giovanna's Ceremony– Sept 23, 2012

GONE! BEFORE THE END OF TIME
Vilanova, shortly after Giovanna's death on August 25, 2012

To have loved again, one so much younger
To find her gone before the end of time
Losing both my loves in just five years
"No, I do not want to love anymore
For then I always suffer."
"No, non vo piu amare
Poiche sempre o a penare."

(Francesco Manelli – from "Acceso mio core"-
"Access to My Heart" translation of two preceding lines.)

Creating your younger self without help
From a negating parental host
Fearless on the ski slope or horseback,
Fearful of failing those you loved -
Wounded more of spirit than body
You succumbed to addiction.

Worrying more for my longevity
Than the damage to loving and living
With the nightmare of your oblivion -
Joy was sucked up by trepidation
For one who played cat-n-mouse with death,
While love held fortress through the turmoil.

Only the finality of seeing
Your own ashes in cloisonné vases
Might have warned you of impending
Doom that would catch you by surprise
Ending your teasing tango with death.
No chance for amending stitch in time.

BY THE RIVER WITH TERRA –
SERENITY AT LAST?
ONLY TIME WILL TELL

As if the tumultuous marriage to Giovanna wasn't enough to brink my passion, a year after her death, I succumbed to the charms of another woman "salvaged by herself" from a literal attic of indifference among her colony of relatives 30 miles away. As the "Cinderella" of the "sisters' hearth," she became relegated to what she could provide in house cleaning chores, baby-sitting, mending and the like.

Moving her away to the freedom of having a house of her own with me, she does not lose the good side of this coterie of local relatives. They begin to see her as an individual instead of "chore girl." Her new independence regains their appreciation for her vibrant character and ability to come up smiling in the face of whatever life dishes out to her.

At age 70, Terra has the flexibility of a ballet dancer, easily getting up from a full crouch on the floor after reading a magazine. Her lithe figure would be the envy of many much younger women, who have to constantly workout to stay in shape. At 5'2" with dark curly hair and a playful spirit, she maintains the exuberance of her childhood, displaying a huge smile that's infectious. Her native intelligence and "street smarts" make up for the education she missed while having to raise her siblings.

Unlike the North Fork of the Snoqualmie River, beside which we live, Terra and I are not resolved to just take what life has to give. We continue to struggle, as in the "Green Kingdom," to make a small difference in our lives rather than letting ourselves become immersed in the occasional floods that have never come into the house since it was built as a log cabin in 1957. We try to give each other a lot of space, along with embracing the warmth of mature love and friendship which doesn't fuss over small things. At times, we say, "Let's forget all that drama. Let it go down the river, so we can focus on *loving again until the end of time.*"

TERRA'S GIFT
Vilanova, written while flying home from NC May 23, 2013

Sharing what we have learned
On this journey though life –
Joined by love not spurned
Day-by-day without strife
What joy Terra gives me:
Another dimension
Beyond solitary -
Green eyes facing the sun,
 She leaves troubles behind
Celebrating the good
That holds the best in mind.
God knows, she understood
What is meant to live with.

TO WIPE AWAY ALL THAT SOOT
Vilanova to Terra – Fall of 2013

Tarratella, sitting by the fireside
A smudge of soot on your nose
Laughing at all those who bide
Their turn to deliver stinging blows
What have all the other ones brought?
No glass slipper to fit your foot
Not the serenity you sought.
To wipe away all that soot,
While giving your own hearth
Your Prince has already come
To enjoy the fire that you kindle
In his loins as well as kingdom.
How perfectly you fit this time
In the balance of his own life –
Beyond compare.

ODE TO TERRA –
GIVING NEW LIFE TO SIMPLE THINGS
Vilanova to Terra while flying home from Houston March 6, 2014

You clothe the table by my chair,
Cinch it with my favorite tie -
Create a turkey tail like fan
Of my Kenyan iv'ry forks
Above a bronze Jesus on cross-
While humming like a busy bee,
Oblivious to solitude.

Have no fear that returning home,
I will but praise your cleverness-
Not minding using fav'rite tie
Lost from my shirt front so long
I had almost forgotten it.
Look for my appreciation
At reviving life's simple things.

MAKING RIVERSIDE SERENITY
Vilanova to Terra in June, 2014

Terra, who made this "terra" her very own,*
No longer fearing the river, only bears,
Consecrating house to our togetherness,
Free as the wild animals she blindly fears,
At last, Terra has journeyed home again.

Sitting with her nephews, Dante and Beau,
We muse upon the "white noise" of the river
Breaking over rapids just a short throw from us,
But turned off as quickly as a light switch
When we go inside and shut the door to it,
So insulated against all that threatens.

Seeing that I am as rooted in her life,
As the hundred-year old riverside maple,
They have opened up to our togetherness –
Rejoicing at what only time can prove
Like the surrounding flowers Terra planted
Paying "home-age" to our shared serenity.

*"terra", as in "terra firma," as arriving at "solid ground" after a stormy sea voyage, a "reliably protective place."

I am sure I will be asked whether, given the chance to go back in time to just after Vernique – would I take the risk of loving again with an ultimate commitment to living together in partnership?

Being happy to have had one great love for most of a lifetime, might I be content to limit myself to friends and family with only the occasional dalliance? Might that not be wise, given the anguish that it is often the coupled to searching for continued fulfillment?

But I cannot give lie to my very nature, the need for intimacy in my life, for the joy that can only come from sharing experience, from waking each morning with my love beside me. So, my answer is an unequivocal "YES," to seeking LOVE AGAIN BEFORE THE END OF TIME.

About VILANOVA DE GAIA

Like Don Quixote, I spent a lifetime tilting at the windmills of love. Becoming an incurable romantic may have sprung from being abandoned for eight years by my mother when I was only four, while growing up in New York City. Although I had many girlfriends, I did not really experience a woman's unreserved reciprocal love until age 25, when I married Vernique in Houston, Texas.

Sent away to a New England boarding school at nine years old, where my entire day was rigidly structured, made me resent any sign of overbearing authority, although my prep-school education did get me into Yale. However, by that time, I had enough of the intense Eastern atmosphere and settled for the University of Texas, where I studied Journalism and Latin American Economic Development. Adventuring in Nicaragua upon graduating, I worked in a gold mine operated by "Rip" Robertson, whom I later found out to be a "rogue" CIA agent, on "leave" for mistakenly blowing up a British, rather than Russian ship off the coast of Nicaragua.

Realizing I wasn't cut out to work for someone else in corporate America, I spent many years operating my own advertising agency in New Orleans, with an emphasis on real estate. Publishing a residential home building magazine, I was called on to publicize the cause for removal of a crooked Director of the local office of the U.S. Dept. of Housing and Urban Development (HUD), whom the government promoted to regional Southwestern Director over Texas and Louisiana after hiding him away in a distant post for a year..

Getting my wife, Vernique, and two children away from the draining heat of the South, I specialized in commercial real estate marketing in Seattle, WA. At the same time, my passion for foreign travel with Vernique led to becoming a wine importer, in which we both received many honors. After her death, I moved to my present riverside home in the mountain foothills, while seeing if I could "love again before the end of time."

Now, Terra and I spend spend more time at home, with enough landscaping and household chores to avoid wasting time over petty personal issues. Since a herd of 300 elk roam the area, there is sufficient wildlife to satisfy my penchant for the African reserves, although Terra is glad not to have encountered a mountain lion or bear.

www.ingramcontent.com/pod-product-compliance
Lightning Source LLC
Chambersburg PA
CBHW070543030426
42337CB00016B/2332